ENDURING:

A Chronological and Personal History of the Carroll College Army ROTC Program

By Nathaniel M. Smith
Completed: 19 APR 2021

Table of Contents

A Note from the Author

This novel captures the history of the military commissioning programs at Carroll College since the college's inception. From its role in both the World Wars to its 21ˢᵗ century establishment, this story attempts to explain what defines Carroll College ROTC.

Upon examination, Carroll College and its SATC Unit, the V-5 & V-12 Naval programs, and the Army ROTC program have conquered objective odds in a variety of fashions to create a longstanding period of success. I named this book, *Enduring: A Chronological and Personal History of The Carroll College Army ROTC Program* to incorporate the evolution of commissioning programs at Carroll College and my own story while in attendance.

The first part of the book is a short, condensed history of the commissioning programs, orchestrated in a chronological timeline. Utilizing interviews, newspaper articles, military logs, and even emails, this history is properly captured in a concise format for prospective students, families, and alumnus of Carroll College. Research on its chronological history was conducted through these available resources with qualitative analysis following. Adding quotes from personal interviews was a credible way to highlight the program's changes and atmosphere at each given period.

Also, my analysis through such sources needed to be confirmed by individuals who were there, the claims I am elaborating upon. I would describe this section as a hybrid between a brochure and a book, tying in personal accounts while giving large quantities of information. The first part of the book is titled: "The Chronological History of CC ROTC."

The second part is my story during the last four years, a first-person account of a cadet's life experiences. My personal history is longer than the first section, attempting to provide greater detail into the thoughts, experiences, and insights I encountered. All the chapters in this section feature a leadership lesson to be derived from my own mistakes and/or from the program overall. Interviews was the primary research tool I included, providing factual basis for my points of self-reflection and individual development.

My personal history is a study on the individual, a study on the existential and physical self in relation to this subject. These methods were chosen carefully to accurately illustrate the changes in an individual over a particular course in time. ROTC is a transitional period where high school graduates are trained to become Army officers. I interpreted this tactic to be well-suited for the subject. An individual in their young adolescence would experience immense change during the duration of programs such as ROTC, prompting my strategy towards the study on the self. The second part of the book is titled: "A Personal History."

The book concludes with a quoted section from former and current military service members as an aid for future Army officers within the program. Additionally, there is a quoted section from the 2021 MSIV class, capturing our insights and advice for future Army officers. Finally, the novel features an appendix, displaying where certain quotes and/or sources of historical information can be found.

The histories of Carroll College's commissioning programs and my own story initially did not strike me with many similarities. I figured that the stories could coincide despite appearing independent, like two stories on different plot lines, told from the same physical setting. Upon my continued research on the subjects, I found that there were many common aspects and relations to one another.

One message I want any readers and future cadets to understand is that our human experience is a challenge. The most important trait I learned while in Saints Company was perseverance. One who endures through the difficulties and insecurities of life can reap great rewards upon conclusion.

If you are going to learn one thing from this book, it's that those who have attended and are currently attending here fight for this program's improvement. Let me spell it out for you: *fighting* means the constant amending and adjusting to this ROTC program's culture and its opportunities. This process includes the strenuous changes necessary for your undertaking, revealing your weaknesses and fears through failure. While ROTC is not the end-state, it is not the ultimate test of your life, it is an opportunity to elevate where you currently stand.

An outlook fashioned this way guarantees success now and in the future. Life in this manner desires a challenge, perceiving *today* as an opportunity. Do not waste your time, you have one guaranteed shot at life—***SEEK & DESTROY!!!***

From the Author,
Nate Smith
06 March 2021

PART I: A Chronological History of CC ROTC

Chapter 1: The Mount St. Charles SATC

As the state of Montana was experiencing rapid growth due to the industrial and agricultural boom, a small, private, Catholic college opened its doors in the state's capital. Carroll College, formerly known as Mount St. Charles College, began to create a curriculum designed to "prepare young men for priesthood and to provide a modern, liberal arts education designed to create numerous career opportunities."[1] The college was primarily established for a catholic based education while promoting religious tolerance: "...allowing students of all faiths and religious sects."[1] Students were required to attend Catholic services while not required to take any courses considering Christian doctrine.

The student population grew at a consistent rate over the college's first decade. Partially influenced by the sudden population and industry development in the state, Helena was an ideal location to establish a small, liberal arts college. Currently, Carroll College is one of three liberal arts colleges in the state, Rocky Mountain College and the University of Montana-Western are the other two. Academic programs, sports, and other extracurricular activities were offered in greater numbers over the College's first period.

Amidst the excitement of the college's growth and expansion, April of 1917 was the time the United States entered the first World War. The student newspaper, *The Prospector* stated: "Patriotism is aflame on Capitol Hill. From the lofty flag pole [which had been erected on campus the year before], Old Glory floats o'er Mount St. Charles College and the boys who are training for their country's service..."[1] Bishop Carroll was concerned over the number of men potentially dropping out to enlist in the war. The College's existence seemed short and negatively affected by the war despite the patriotism among student and faculty members.[1]

Next, Bishop Carroll requested for Mount St. Charles to be permitted as a Student Army Training Corps (SATC) site to help mitigate losing students from the draft. Upon acceptance, Mount St. Charles was the only catholic college in the country to be approved as an SATC host school. The SATC's duration at Carroll was rather brief, only existing for about a month before "...news of the armistice reached Helena and the rest of the United States" on November 11th of 1918.[1] The Mount St. Charles SATC unit had 131 students join the program, a large number attending, especially considering the program lasted for about a month's time.

World War I did not last long enough for it to effect Mount St. Charles' future as a young college. Yet, "...it did help to set a precedent for cooperation between the school and the nation's military services, a relationship that would profoundly affect the college in the next world war."[1]

In the following years before World War II, there was no military officer training units of any kind on campus. The young college saw professional and architectural development following the

SATC's disbandment. Architectural developments include the construction of a new St. Charles Hall on top of capitol hill, a library, chapel, auditorium, dining room, kitchen, and gymnasium.[1] For about thirty years, Mount St. Charles "...made arrangements with the Sisters of St. Dominic in Speyer, Germany, to bring nuns to the college."[1]

A quote from a historian discussing this change to the young college wrote, "Bishop Carroll's offer of employment convinced the sisters to embark on a journey that would separate them from their country, kin, and motherhouse. Not only did the sisters view America as the 'Land of Unlimited Opportunities,' but their spirit of determination to aid the motherhouse prompted them to venture into the 'Wilds of America.'"[1] Mount St. Charles constructed the Sisters of St. Dominic a new residence (Saint Albert's today), to be their new convent. The Sisters' presence at the college helped establish early academic success and helped elevate the spiritual and educational curriculum overall.[1]

In 1919, Mount St. Charles was officially credited by the North Central Association of Colleges and Secondary Schools. The newly found organization "...helped maintain uniformity and quality standards in American Education" and eased the accreditation of academic programs at the college.[1] By 1932, "...the college's baccalaureate-degree programs had been officially accredited" and Mount St. Charles was voted to be renamed as Carroll College in honor of its founder, Bishop Carroll.[1] Through the 1930s, the college had difficulty increasing enrollment during the Great Depression. This caused tremendous financial difficulties for the college having about half of their attendance in the 1920s.[1]

Following the rejuvenation of the American economy, Carroll's attendance began to increase yet again. In the fall of 1941, immediately preceding World War II, the college's attendance stood at 134 students.[1] As World War II began, Carroll's faculty and leadership were concerned over the number of college students and faculty members rushing to join military service.[1] Carroll's financial issues and concerns over the declining attendance rate compelled the college to seek federal funding, similar to many small, private colleges and universities across the country.

The federal government was now involved in the war, neglecting the budget issues of institutions such as Carroll. Concerned over the lack of officers in the Army and Navy, the present needs of the college and the federal government seemed to coincide. Similar to Bishop Carroll's request for Mount St. Charles to become a SATC institution in World War I, the establishment of an officer training corps during World War II would "...bring together the benefit for both" for the armed services and America's colleges.

Chapter 2: The Good Ship Carroll

On February 26, 1943, a photograph was taken of the class of 70 aviation cadets enrolled for ground instruction at Carroll and flight instruction at the Morrison Flying Service.[2] Until 1939, Carroll had trained over 300 pilots through the civilian Pilot Training Program. At the time, Carroll College was an All-Navy school for the exclusive basic training of naval aviation cadets until the Navy Department's appointment for the V-12 program in November, 1942.[3]

The V-5 program was an aviation training program, consisting of war training service (WTS) flight prep for the second world war.[2] The newly established V-12 aimed at commissioning new naval officers, started following the V-5. On April 30th of that year, Carroll was accepted by the Navy, increasing its yearly attendance through 300 incoming "bluejackets" and 70 aviation cadets for the V-12.[5]

From 1943 to 1945, the *Good Ship Carroll* housed 704 V-12 trainees, arguably saving Carroll from shutting down for a lack of students, due to Carroll being an all-male institution.[5] Units like Carroll's V-12 were placed at about 125 colleges during the war, the Montana School of Mines (Montana Tech) is another such example. Most V-12 candidates were seventeen and eighteen years old, coming right out of high school. The remainder of the program consisted of fleet men from other Navy duty stations and ships.

V-12 servicemen would be enrolled in a basic college course as "apprentice seamen", consisting of a basic college course of about 20 hours a week, in four-month semesters, for about 16 months total.[5] Curriculum comprised of the basic preparatory course for naval officer candidates. V-12 education included the proper way to salute, march, wear a uniform, naval verbiage, intense spot checks, and swift punishment for disobeying orders. One such experience was from Ed Rosendahl, who performed "extensive tooth-brush cleaning of fifth deck baseboards after Chief McShane (E7) got me for some infraction."[6] Cadets were placed under the teachings and responsibilities of Naval officers and NCOs. Lieutenant David McDonald (O3) was appointed as the commanding officer of the newly established program with Lieutenant (j.g., O2) Merle J. Ririe as the executive officer. In addition, Ensign Ann Graham (O1) was the disbursing officer and Lieutenant Commander Rutz was the program's medical officer. Following cadre members were Chief Specialist John J. McShane, three storekeepers (supply technicians and record keeping NCOs), one yeoman (cleric and general administrative NCO), and one pharmacist's mate (medical care).[4]

By August of 1943, two hundred and fifty-four V-12 trainees (121 from California and 78 from Montana) were in the program.[4] The two hundred and fifty-four V-12 trainees were divided into three companies: C on fifth deck, B on fourth deck, and A on third deck. A V-5 Wing house separated aviation cadets from the rest of the program.

V-5 candidates had an entirely different unit organization and schedule from the V-12 program. No classes were held with the V-5 and V-12 trainees together. One former V-5 member "does not recall having met one of them."[2] V-5 curriculum was comprised of learning to fly and solo T-crafts, open cockpit N3N bi-planes, and receiving continuous flight instruction from the Morrison Flying Service.[2]

Less than a month later, Naval regulations improved Carroll College's facilities to be up to standard with Naval requirements for V-12 trainees.[4] November 1st of 1943 was the arrival of fifty-eight new V-12 trainees, featuring 41 from the civilian sector and 17 from the fleet. By May of 1944, fifty-two trainees were scheduled to complete the V-12 course and 140 new trainees were reporting to Carroll that upcoming July. A majority of these new arrivals were V-12A candidates while the remainder were pre-medical, and pre-dental students.

-

Much of the college's clergymen and faculty members embraced the rigorous standards set by the *Good Ship Carroll*. One example was math professor, Father Topel, who would "leave the classroom windows open during Winter, in case a sailor would nod off."[6] The academic, military, and physical standards of Carroll College and the V-12 program made time-management a priority among trainees.

Physical training for the V-12 program included a structured obstacle course—swinging ropes, ladders, brick walls, and 16 other barriers built on a 440-yard track.[4] V-12 trainees were required to spend an hour and a half each day conducting strenuous physical activities. Physical activities included calisthenics, basketball, soccer, gymnastics, and tumbling. Carroll's football coach, Ed Simonich, a former star of Notre Dame, was put in charge of physical fitness for the trainees. Wartime restrictions prohibited V-12 members from playing college football but the Fighting Saints Basketball team had a vast amount of success during this period. After the decommissioning of the programs, "Two members of the 1944-45 team went on to play varsity basketball for the University of Colorado..."[5] In February of 1945, Carroll and the School of Mines in Butte (Montana Tech) shared a basketball title because their tie record was not played off.[5]

Despite the difficulties set by the V-5 & V-12 cadre and Carroll's faculty, much of the townspeople and businesses in Helena enjoyed having the "men in blue" in town. The Parrot, a local confectionary still operating today, was a social setting for trainees to enjoy refreshments, ice cream, and for meeting local girls.[2] Amidst the V-12's newfound presence, the 1st Special Forces group was also stationed at Fort Harrison, near downtown Helena, having a profound impact on locals during the war period. Similarly, the college was positively impacted by the program's presence and vice versa. Townspeople held parties and "provided these young men opportunities to socialize with young women."[6] Helena households routinely invited trainees into their homes for dinners during the week and for the holidays.

The Navy held dances during the program's duration, "utilizing the instrumental and vocal talents of some of the sailors."[6] In addition, the V-12 had trainees involved in dance band, marching band, the school newspaper, and a men's glee club.

-

The V-5 naval aviation program closed on August 5th of 1944 (about two months after the D-Day invasion).[4] By October, seventy-five trainees were to transfer to other V-12 or Naval ROTC units. The V-12's 120 second and fifth term men remaining were to be joined by about 80 men from the fleet. The second world war ended in August of 1945, prompting the Navy to reduce the number of pilots needed. Programs like Carroll's V-12 were soon shut down, all candidates were dispersed as needed.[3]

Dispersed trainees had to choose whether to remain in the program, gaining a commission as a Naval officer (three years on active-duty orders) or go "general duty" in the Navy. General duty's requirements were fulfilled upon former trainees' accumulation of enough "discharge points" to be eligible to be separated from service.[2]

About a year later, the Naval V-12 program was decommissioned on November 27th, 1945. One hundred and seventeen seamen were transferred to other NROTC units at the end of the semester, 15 became civilians upon the program's shutdown. Transferred trainees were to go to the University of Washington (36 apprentice seamen) and the University of Colorado (81).[4] Fourteen pre-medical students were to go on inactive duty, free to continue their education at the schools of their choice. One trainee was discharged under the point system.

After the war, many former members of Carroll's V-12 program entered careers in: engineering, medicine, government service, real estate, ranching, education, law, journalism, manufacturing, and other fields of employment.[6] About twenty-five from the V-5/V-12 programs held bilennial reunions until a few years past 2002.[5] Many remained close regardless of their lives after Carroll. No ROTC or military commissioning program of any kind was present at Carroll College until the early 2000s.

Chapter 3: Early Days

On May 9th, 2003, 2LT Jason R. Brockus became the first commissioned officer out of the Carroll Army ROTC program.[9] Since the decommissioning of the V-5 and V-12 programs, no military commissioning programs of any kind were present on the Carroll College campus. MAJ Nugent and MSG Duezabou were the first cadre appointed upon the program's inception.[9] The formation of the ROTC attachment at Carroll seems almost sudden and abrupt.

-

Carroll College's ROTC program is staffed and funded by the Montana Army National Guard (MTARNG) as a development channel for future officers.[9] Upon creation in the fall of 2001, ROTC came to Carroll as a satellite program to the University of Montana. Former comments made by MAJ Patrick Nugent highlighted the goals of the program, "...the program's primary objective is to prepare academically and physically qualified college women and men for the rigor and challenge of serving as officers in the U.S. Army."[12]

ROTC's establishment at Carroll was a joint effort between the MTARNG, the college, and the Diocese of Helena.[11] MTARNG committed to two soldiers to help facilitate and Carroll was to provide academic resources and a secretary for recruiting, classroom instruction, office space, and a vehicle.[11] Key individuals in ROTC's inception at Carroll include Major General Gene Pendergast (TAG-MTARNG) and Dr. Tom Trebon (Carroll President).[11]

The original campus ROTC office was located on the "sub-main in St. Charles Hall...offering two and four-year programs."[12] ROTC scholarship benefits were similar to their current state, offering to pay all tuition fees (at the time only $16,000 annually without room and board), a book stipend, and a monthly stipend for contracted Cadets. In its first year, the corps of cadets was comprised of only six individuals.[11]

Initial issues in the program's establishment were in the proper funding of the program's costs and gaining traction within the college's community: "Carroll's ROTC program needed full tuition scholarships in order to attract recruits, Cadet Command was reluctant to give out so many scholarships."[11]

A former cadre member and one of the first cadets at Carroll College, CPT Mark Thompson of the MTARNG, describes the program during its early years: "Upon creation, Carroll applied UM's methods to recreate their success...The Montana Guard took great care of the program, providing training opportunities and materials necessary for us. We had a lot of prior service cadets who had greater experience and were older than they are now. In fact, only one or two had no prior experience to the military."[13]

Despite having some initial support by a portion of the campus community, the program was not accepted by the entirety of Carroll College. For example, military science (physical training or MSL) did not count as academic credit for the first 3-4 years upon the program's establishment.[15] Initial recruits had to pay out of pocket to have an opportunity to compete for a scholarship. Additionally, the program still lacked size, being only a satellite program comprised of only eight cadets entirely.[15] Platoon leadership labs (usually done in the spring semester) could only be practiced by about the size of a squad, forcing "creativity" and "innovation" during training events.

Furthermore, Carroll's student demographic has a fairly limited veteran community, most students are eighteen years old while starting their freshman year.[15] In order to mitigate this issue, Cadre former cadre members CPT Kostecki and CW2 Bollinger (formerly LTCOL) had to educate the faculty about what ROTC was, what the Army leadership training model meant, and the opportunities offered to Cadets while in ROTC.[15]

A notable example was a nursing cadet who recieved an offer to shadow a combat medic in Germany, offering casualty trauma care to wounded soldiers in combat zones. This training experience had a profound impact on this cadet, "shaping her perspective on her military service overall."[15] The presentation of her training experience helped gain positive exposure for the program, simultaneously showing the applicability of her education. Faculty members were amazed by her experiences, stories like hers was one method ROTC became fully integrated into the Carroll College community. Additionally, according to the first OIC of Carroll's ROTC Program, COL Patrick Nugent (Retired), cadets maintained positive relationships with the staff, bringing the faculty's support towards the Army and the ROTC program.[11]

Other problems arose during its early years, constricting the growth of Carroll's ROTC program. For example, the opposing priorities between the National Guard and Cadet Command on Carroll's officer production.[15] The National Guard desired Carroll cadets to commission directly into the National Guard, due to a need of officers throughout the state of Montana. Typically, Carroll has commissioned officers into National Guard units at a rate of about 50% per commissioning class, 25% being the national average.[15] Usually commissioning classes at Carroll consist of about 6-10 cadets. On average, Carroll produces at least three National Guard officers every year.

Even in the spring class of 2021, Cadets Trevor Drinville and Zach Brandt will commission into the MTARNG in May of 2021. Drinville and Brandt were SMP cadets (members of MTARNG) during their ROTC curriculum at Carroll. In my MSIV class, the MSIVs graduating later in 2021 or in 2022 will most likely commission into the National Guard or Army Reserves (3 total). Out of my class of eight cadets, it is probable that only three will commission into Active-Duty units. This is contrary to the

University of Montana's spring of 2021 commissioning class, where eleven out of eleven will commission into full time positions in Active-Duty forces.

-

Cadet Command is federally funded, justifying their allocation of military and financial resources with different priorities than the MTARNG.[15] Shortly after its establishment, Carroll's ROTC program was almost shut down due to the college not producing enough nursing officers. Attributed to its prestige as a nursing school, Cadet Command saw Carroll College as a worthwhile investment because it had a shortage of nurses in active-duty components.[15] It is worth mentioning that nursing cadets commission directly into active units. Being a smaller school at an attendance of about 1,200 students every year, a smaller ROTC program would not be a burden to the budget, due to the nursing program's recognition.[15]

Moreover, the maximum carrying capacity of Carroll's ROTC program was set to a limit of 40 cadets.[15] In order to ensure the existence of Saints Company, early cadre members focused their efforts on commissioning nursing officers because the program required both state and federal funding.[14] If nursing officers could commission, Carroll could still receive federal funds while continuously commissioning officers into the MTARNG.

Yet, the Montana Army National Guard and Cadet Command's higher-ranking officials were still in constant dispute over the purpose of Carroll's ROTC program. Due to this conflict, from 2004-2005 no new scholarships were given to cadets at Carroll.[15] The lack of funding made recruiting quite difficult but all currently contracted cadets still maintained scholarship benefits from 2004-2005.[15]

In 2005, a large amount of money suddenly went towards the military caused by the wars in Iraq and Afghanistan rapidly escalating.[15] Almost overnight, scholarships were easily accessible, increasing recruitment, retention, and success overall within the young program. Former OIC and current CW2 Bollinger illustrates the ease of awarding scholarships to uncontracted cadets: "If a member of the ROTC program fulfilled the minimum requirements of a 2.0 GPA, could pass the fitness test, and met all legal and medical qualifications, money was easily available to award that individual a two-to-five years of contract benefits."[15]

Over the duration of CW2 Bollinger's career at Carroll, the ROTC program grew from eight to thirty cadets. One effect of the program's rapid growth was the age and experience of its cadets. Early on, Carroll's cadets were typically men and women of prior service, older than the typical age of Carroll's students.[15] Upon expansion, most of Carroll's cadets were joining ROTC at eighteen or nineteen years old, having no previous experience in the military.

Another effect was the strengthening of relationships among Carroll's cadets. Attributed partially to its establishment and expansion, Saints Company typically has a stronger relationship among its members than most ROTC programs.[13] According to CW2 Bollinger, "Most of Carroll's cadets were tighter knit than other programs due to shared interests, experiences, and backgrounds. The typical applicant to Carroll chooses Carroll over other colleges or universities due to its close community and academic standards."[15]

An example of Carroll's community is seen in the story of a former Cadet Kally Keppet, a current SARC officer in the MTARNG. Keppet was born in the Netherlands and naturalized as a United States citizen during her time in ROTC. All of Carroll's cadre members and most of the program's cadets attended her naturalization, she contracted the following day.[15] Kally Keppet has worked key full-time positions in the MTARNG, working in the TAG program, having a successful military career in a variety of manners.

Around 2004-2005, the change in the demographic within the Carroll's structure formed a certain contrast within Grizzly Battalion. The University of Montana (UM) is a state funded university, usually having an attendance of around 15,000 students per year. Most cadets from UM are typically older with more cadets having prior service backgrounds. By 2004-2005, Montana had a program size of about 75 cadets. Some UM cadets had "combat experience, came from non-traditional backgrounds, and even one cadet was on the state legislature."[15]

UM's program was very well established by this point in time. It was supported and staffed with multiple Active-Duty Officers, NCOs, and Army Civilians.[11] At Carroll, there was only one OIC, one NCOIC, and one secretary. This difference placed much of the stress and necessary tasks for Carroll's young ROTC program upon three individuals compared to multiple staff members at UM. Carroll's program has always been "cadet run".[11] A smaller program requires a greater amount of individual responsibility for cadets because of its lack of resources and staff.

The objective differences between Carroll College and the University of Montana have formed "friendly competition" between the two schools.[13] Most notably, competing for company PT scores and during training events such as FTX, rifle qualification, or Cadet Summer Training (CST).[15] A banter between the schools cyclically erupts and erodes during each school year. In the past, acts of stealing company guidons and minor vandalism have occurred either in Schreiber Gym or at Carroll's ROTC house. Notably, sardines were littered throughout the ROTC house my freshman year, resulting in 24/7 staff duty assignments for Carroll's cadets.

Typically, such examples are the extent of the friendly feud between the schools. Tensions between cadre and/or cadet members of either institution are redirected to avenues of competition, attempting to elevate the performance of the battalion as a whole.

-

Similar to today, many cadets are rewarded with additional training opportunities due to merit within the program. Cadet Dan Synness was the first cadet from Carroll College to attend the Army Basic Airborne Course in Fort Benning, Georgia in July of 2002.[16] The Basic Airborne course has been in existence for about 80 years, hosting most branches of military service for specialized training, allowing a candidate to "earn their wings".[16] The prestigious school received significant recognition through the valor displayed by units like the 101st and 82nd Airborne during World War II.

The second cadet to attend the Airborne course was Cadet Phil Kilbreath in May of 2003.[7] Having cadets attend Airborne school and additional Army schools helped the program gain recognition and respect around the school during its early years.[15] Furthermore, Cadet Dan Synness was recognized as a member of Carroll's Dean List in the fall semester of 2001, the first cadet from the program to do so.[8] Professionalism, academic excellence, and individual determination has been apparent in Carroll's ROTC program throughout its existence.

Carroll's previous programs in the first and second World Wars adds another dimension to the program's history of success. As illustrated by *The Good Ship Carroll*, Carroll College developed another avenue for its students to pursue and excel in military service. To these cadets who exemplify the perseverance of Carroll's predecessors, additional Army training opportunities are offered during college. Air Assault, Jungle School, Mountain Warfare, and Diving School(s) have been attended by current and/or past cadets within Saints Company.

-

Following the program's creation, ROTC at Carroll featured FTXs, land navigation, combat water training, and organized community events similar to today. Minor differences to today include cadets' participation in leadership reaction courses, scenarios designed to aid in a unit's cohesion when given a difficult task to complete.[7] Previously, land navigation featured a 3-point compass course contrary to its standards today. Instruction on building rope bridges used to be provided during FTXs and leadership labs.

Today, the program conducts a combat water survival test (CWST). The CWST is a "go" or "no-go" event, only needed to be successfully completed once in a cadet's duration in ROTC. Previously, the CWST was called "drown-proofing".[7] The CWST in the past featured the same events as it does currently: an underwater load-bearing vest (LBV or LCE) drop, jumping off of a diving board while maintaining control of your rifle, and three other swimming tests.[7]

FTXs during the fall and spring were slightly different compared to FTXs in 2021. For about the first eight years, Carroll participated with the University of Montana and Officer Candidates (OCS) from MTARNG during field training exercises.[7] "Cadets were trained on Night and Day Land Navigation,

Squad Situation Training Exercises, and the Field Leaders Reactions Course, and a 6.2-mile forced ruck march with rucksacks."[7]

My freshman year, in the spring of 2018, FTX consisted of rucking to and from lanes, setting up a patrol base upon day's end, and concluding with an 8-mile ruck march. Throughout my first spring FTX, Grizzly Battalion traveled 32 miles by means of rucking throughout the weekend. Land navigation is typically completed during the fall FTX. Usually before land navigation, squads go through the obstacle course and repel tower at Fort Harrison.

Cadets were also given prior instruction on the M16A2 rifle before rifle qualification in the early 2000s. At the time, rifle qualification consisted of a 40 round qualification course at the pop-up target range at Fort Harrison.[10] Today, rifle qualification consists of six tables: an ammo identification quiz, preliminary marksmanship instruction (PMI), laser bore-sighting the M4A1 rifle; electronic simulator qualification; zeroing the M4A1 with a red dot sight (CCO); a confirmation of your zero on the pop-up range; and two marksmanship courses, including moving and reloading between firing positions (40 rounds per table). In all FTXs, rifles are cleaned at the end of training and/or rifle qualification.[10] After shooting, cleaned rifles must be cleared by a cadre member to pass in accordance to Army standards.

In the past three years, rifles are issued during FTXs with blanks to make training exercises as realistic as possible. This was established to give MSIIIs practice with creating an ammo plan for their Platoon in preparation for CST. Live ammunition forces cadets to adhere to improved rifle handling and etiquette. Additionally, it teaches the proper loading, reloading, and clearing procedures on the M16A2, M4A1, M249 SAW, and M240B weapons systems.

Chapter 4: Preceding the Unknown

In 2012, SFC Robert Cassidy (SSG) arrived at Carroll College as the new NCOIC for the Carroll ROTC program. At the time, Saints Company recently made a few changes, making the program resemble closer to what it is today. First, the current headquarters of Saints Company was recently established at its current home on Euclid Avenue. A humble, older, 1970s style home became a perfect cove for cadets' classes, meetings, and homework.

Additionally, Mrs. Janet Sheehy became the program's secretary between the College and the ROTC program. The secretary answers any questions or concerns regarding academic and commissioning necessities. Saints Company was also recognized for multiple years for having a nationally and regionally successful ROTC program. Finally, ROTC at Carroll concluded its duration of doing physical fitness training at the athletic facilities' basketball courts, moving PT sessions to the Haunthausen Athletic Center (HAC).

Former Cadets describe the program's environment before and during Sergeant Cassidy's tenure as rigorous, challenging, and demanding.[18] MS1 cadets were expected to heavily direct and teach military science classes and lead during morning PT sessions. This change in program culture directly translated to applications during lab. MS1 & MS2 cadets assumed greater responsibilities and experience in leadership positions, raising the expectations of younger cadets within the program.[19]

Saints Company's cadre continued the standards outlined by previous cadre members, attempting to elevate all aspects of performance within ROTC cadets. SFC Robert Cassidy described the program's previous environment as, "I think the predecessor had a similar attitude as I, the program seemed to be heading in the right direction. I wanted to apply my own twist on leadership and development among cadets. We seemed to flourish during my tenure here and I think that's due to a commitment to excellence from cadre and cadets."[17]

Cadets regularly attended Army training schools such as Airborne or Air Assault and opportunities abroad through the CULP program. Carroll's curriculum still maintained a high degree of academic challenges, prompting cadre to help fix any academic or personal issues affecting performance.[17] Cadre's primary objective during this time was to prepare cadets with little to no prior service experience to become competent enough to lead soldiers in any capacity in the Army.[17] SFC Cassidy and CPT Thompson's combat arms backgrounds gave valuable insight for cadets while cadre members from 2012-2019.[18]

-

The program's size went back and forth during this period, fluctuating from about twenty to over thirty cadets. The demographics of cadets remained relatively the same. Most cadets were from Montana, Idaho, Washington, and other western states. In the previous commissioning class (2020), there were four cadets total. Two were from Washington, one from Montana, and one from Colorado. In the spring of 2021, five cadets will commission. Three are from Montana, one from Colorado, and one from Washington (myself). Throughout both of classes most cadets have not had any prior military experience before ROTC.

-

Saints Company became a desirable place for prospective students due to the success stories of previous cadets. This led to a significant growth period overall, a result attributed to the support of the University of Montana's cadre members, mainly its Professors of Military Science (PMS).[17] Mrs. Janet Sheehy also developed a continuity and improved relations between the Carroll faculty and ROTC program. Moreover, cadre desired to interact often with students, furthering Carroll's tight-knit community. CPT Thompson being a Carroll alumnus promoted this notion, a selling point for the program's recruiting and community.[17]

A smaller ROTC program elevated cadets' accomplishments and improvements over their college careers, making each experience more meaningful. Essentially, this transitional period, ROTC, became important to a small group of cadre members, faculty, and students due to the program's members proximity to one another. A positive public reputation had already been established. Now, its reputation needed to be maintained, aiming to improve each year.

Upon expansion, students on campus saw a greater impact of cadets within the college community. Cadets were more commonly seen in uniform at campus, serving in student government positions, involved in clubs, and participating in college athletics.[15] Such exposure gave more positive recognition to the successes of current and former cadets. Saints Company's newfound responsibility of meeting the program's expectations prompted the emphasis of professionalism, academic success, and commitment from all of its cadets.

Cadets yearned for elevating the successes of the program, trying to provide a positive image for the college as a whole. Former Cadre OIC, CPT Mark Thompson said, "Cadets continue to improve the program. ROTC's expansion allows a greater picture on campus; students want to be here so it all took care of itself. Our product had to be good enough to handoff to Captain Clark upon my departure...It was very difficult to leave Carroll, I loved this job."[13]

In addition, Carroll's ROTC program still required awarding scholarships to prospective cadets. Many ROTC programs were being cut nationwide in the early 2010s.[17] Maintaining strong attendance and success across all MS-levels became necessary for the program's survival. Like its predecessors, the SATC and V-5/V-12 programs, the aftermath of large-scale conflicts often lead to the reduction in military commissioning programs. With policy changes towards the Army's interests in Iraq in Afghanistan during this period, ROTC units like Carroll were endangered despite its accomplishments.

Resilience through these difficult and challenging circumstances further defined the program and its members. Whether through the means of tougher expectations or reputation of Carroll ROTC graduates, the small, liberal arts college in Helena not only survived but prospered immensely.

Moreover, the trajectory of the program's survival and success was influenced by cadre members in Missoula. At the time, the Professor of Military Science, LTC Chad Carlson and Battalion NCOIC, MSG Jeremy Dose offered different methods on the proper teaching, training, and mentorship of cadets. Challenges were established on a daily quota, cadets were forced to earn results, respect, and recognition every single day. In the words of current 2nd LT Parker Perry (Class of '20), "Your reputation started at day one, you could not show weakness (in a positive way). You needed to perform at the highest level...I learned a lot about myself during my first year at Carroll."[18]

As previously stated, a crucial objective for Grizzly Battalion was and still is developing effective officers for all scopes of the Army.[17] Responsibilities towards your soldiers and commitment to accomplishing the mission was taught from day one. Another way to characterize this period compared to its early years was the enhancement of its military curriculum. The ability to work as a member of a team, developing competent decision making, and self-accountability were progressively incorporated into a cadet's life in ROTC. Training exercises were now focused around a MSIII's success at Cadet Summer Training (CST), raising the expectations yet again.

Every year, the senior leadership has to create more innovative scenarios and labs for proficient training. Over time, the performance levels among cadets and its required curriculum was upgraded incrementally in this small, competitive ROTC program.

-

It is common for cadets, in particular, to become distracted by college life and personal issues. The curriculum had to be structured towards meeting the needs of cadets while properly evolving them into Army officers.[17] Current 2nd LT, Otis Smith (Class of '20) described the Captain Thompson and Sergeant Cassidy era as, "It was very NCO led, you were required to do all the right things. Your formations had to be correct, your tasks had to be thoroughly completed, and there was a large emphasis on discipline."[19]

The process of training a successful cadet is quite difficult. At the command level, it was arduous to balance the differing objectives of the MTARNG and Cadet Command while addressing the personal needs of young adults. Retention among its members is often challenging when emphasizing discipline and rigorous responsibilities. Cadets are being developed from the end of high school to their commissioning date, requiring a drastic learning curve over four years. "They come in as young 17–18-year old's trying to join a program they may or may not know anything about…I applaud all the soldiers who worked their butts off. The growth is monumental and necessary for the world and the Army. Levels of Physical health, intellect, and confidence improve incredibly from arriving to their commissioning date."[17]

-

Without the work of their predecessors, the cadre members and cadets of Saints Company could not be where it is today. The prowess of the program was clear upon my arrival. Cadets of all MS-levels appeared richened with experiences, making them stand a little taller. I was quickly impressed with my peers and cadre members.

At the first circle-up on my first day in college, I possessed the urge to impress the individuals I was greatly intimidated by. It reminded me a lot of high school sports, where you come in to that first meeting as a bug-eyed freshman. Everyone sizes you up, making rapid judgements over who you are and how well you can play. Similar to then, I wanted to have the right answer for everything asked of me. *I felt my legs begin to twitch and shake; the words that came out of my mouth fell to the floor like drool.* Their expectations of me were clearly defined right off the bat, I was excited for this new beginning but humbled in its initial process.

CHRONOLOGY OF THE U. S. NAVY AT CARROLL COLLEGE, HELENA, MONTANA, IN WORLD WAR II

As Reported in THE PROSPECTOR, Student Newspaper

Compiled by Paul Verdon, A.S., V-12A, U.S.N.R.
Of the Crew of the GOOD SHIP CARROLL

FEBRUARY 26, 1943--A photograph of the current class of 70 aviation cadets enrolled for ground instruction at Carroll with flight instruction at Morrison Flying Service. Carroll had trained over 300 pilots since 1939 through the Civilian Pilot Training Program and was designated as an All-Navy School for the exclusive basic training of naval aviation cadets in November, 1942.

MARCH 26, 1943--Carroll was placed on the first approved list of colleges and universities for possible contract by the Navy Department for V-12 Program. About 125 institutions were approved.

APRIL 30, 1943--Carroll was accepted by the Navy and 300 bluejackets and 70 aviation cadets were expected when Carroll opened July 1, 1943. The V-12 men would be on active duty as apprentice seamen and would be enrolled in a basic college course of about 20 hours a week and would remain the program for four-month semesters for about 16 months. The curriculum would be the basic preparatory course for naval officer candidates. Navy officers would be charge. During the past month a detachment of aviation cadets arrived from Ohio Wesleyan Pre-Flight School at Delaware, Ohio, for advanced ground instruction and flight training. During the past month, 13 men earned solo wing pins.

MAY 21, 1943--An obstacle course of swinging ropes, ladders, brick walls, and 16 other barriers was built on the 440-yard track. V-12 trainees were to spend 1½ hour a day in strenuous athletics: calisthenics, basketball, soccer, gymnastics, and tumbling with Carroll's football coach, Ed Simonich, a former Notre Dame star, in charge.

Military log of the U.S. Navy at Carroll College during the tenure of the V-5 and V-12 commissioning Programs. Compiled by former V-12A seaman, Paul Verdon of The *Good Ship Carroll*.

Courtesy of the Carroll College Military Science Department

Photograph of the V-5 Aviation detachment class. Taken for *The Prospector* newspaper in 1943.

Courtesy of the Carroll College Military Science Department

Jason Brockus, the first student commissioned as a 2nd Lt. in the Carroll College ROTC program, looks to his future in Fort Benning, Ga., where he will begin active duty in the summer of 2003.

Eliza Wiley
IR Staff Photographer

Photograph of Jason Brockus, the first commissioned 2LT from the Carroll College Army ROTC program. Taken in 2003 for the *Independent Record* newspaper.

Courtesy of the Carroll College Military Science Department

Newspaper article from *The Prospector* released in 2002, about two years after ROTC's establishment.

Courtesy of the Carroll College Military Science Department

CARROLL COLLEGE PROSPECTOR   NEWS   Mon. Feb. 11th 2002   5

Vol 85 No. 4

Army ROTC program up and running at Carroll

By Austin Mapston
Staff reporter

The Carroll College Army ROTC program, a relatively new addition to Carroll College, is nearing its one-year anniversary.

From its inception last winter, the ROTC program has seen a great amount of interest.

Currently there are 10 cadets, five males and five females, with hopes to increase those numbers next year. Master Sgt. John Duezabou and Maj. Pat Nugent instruct the program.

Nugent said that the cadets in the Carroll College ROTC program are pursuing 4-year degrees in fields ranging from nursing and biology, to business administration and pre-law, to education and environmental studies.

In addition to general college studies and courses, cadets also participate in military science classroom courses, in which they study military history, leadership principles, management techniques, public speaking skills, decision-making processes, problem-solving techniques, and physical training procedures.

Cadets in the ROTC program train to become officers in the Army, Army National Guard, or Army Reserve.

Those who participate in the program may be awarded a full tuition and fees scholarship as well as a monthly stipend to cover room and board expenses as they are not covered in the scholarship.

Cadets participate in various training exercises that include learning to swim and survive in water while sporting an M16 and all other necessary gear.

Cadets also undertake various field exercises such as team building obstacle courses and live ammunition practice at Fort Harrison in Helena.

"We help people realize their full potential," said Duezabou. "We motivate people to do things that they never thought they were capable of doing. While in training, cadets may scale a wall to help overcome their fear of heights or jump blindfolded off a diving board into a pool to help overcome their fear of the unknown. All of these help them do things that they never thought they could."

Cadet Cpl. Daniel Synness said that the most challenging aspect of the program was, "achieving success while maintaining a full class load while taking a rigorous physical and academic program."

Synness, a former National Guard Pfc., now a freshman busi-

I HAVE MADE FIRE: Carroll College Army ROTC cadets join forces with cadets from the University of Montana during a recent training excursion into the wilderness.

ness administration major from Helena, said that he would, "recommend the ROTC program to anyone who wants a rewarding challenge."

"I joined the ROTC for financial assistance, adventure, leadership training, and the wonderful opportunities the ROTC program offers. The ROTC program has had a tremendous impact on me. Without the ROTC scholarship I would not be able to afford to go to Carroll," said Cadet Jaylynn Parcel, a freshman from Fairfield, Mont., who is majoring in chemistry for secondary education.

Those students who still have at least two years of college left may

take advantage of all that the ROTC has to offer.

To be accepted into the ROTC advanced course, students must have either been to basic training, had previous military experience, attended Basic Camp- a training program in Fort Knox, Ky.- or have had two years of enrollment in a ROTC program Nugent explained.

For more information about the Carroll College Army ROTC program contact Master Sgt. John Duezabou at 447-5487, or Maj. Pat Nugent at 447-5487. Students can also stop by the ROTC office on campus, located on the first floor of St. Charles

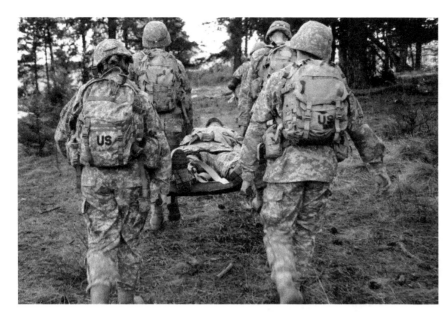

Carroll cadets carrying a wounded cadet using a SKEDCO during Leadership Lab.

Courtesy of the Carroll College Military Science Department

A cadet going down the repel tower at Fort Harrison during Fall FTX, 2017. It is common for cadets to get quite nervous before their first repel, often leading to a poorly tied Swiss-Seat. I learned the hard way on my first swiss-seat...

Courtesy of the Carroll College Military Science Department

Grizzly Battalion gathered around at the terrain model for the first day of Fall FTX, 2017. I only remember arriving there at 0500, freezing my butt off waiting for four more hours before we got started. *"Hurry Up and Wait"* I guess.

Courtesy of the Carroll College Military Science Department

Cadets exiting out of the CH-47 Chinook helicopter at the start of Fall FTX, 2017 at Fort Harrison.

Courtesy of the Carroll College Military Science Department

Cadet Travis Petersen during a PLT Recon Lab, Spring 2020. Taken one week before COVID-19 closed Carroll College.

Courtesy of the Carroll College Military Science Department

My friends and I at our High School Graduation at Eastside Catholic High School, June of 2017.

Pictured (from left to right): Dylan Feldhaus, Christian Amador, Cam Lakes, Tyler Folkes, Chris Lefau, myself, and Koa Roberts

Courtesy of Michael Smith

Most of the Class of 2021 during our MS1 year. Taken during Spring FTX, 2018.

Pictured (from left to right): Trevor Drinville, Daniel Guthrie, Dathan Bicoy, Tori Lahrman, Jacob Rasch, Zach Brandt, and myself

Courtesy of the Carroll College Military Science Department

Carroll's Class of 2021 at Dining Out our Sophomore year (MS2). Taken in February, 2019.

Top-row: Daniel Guthrie, Trevor Drinville, Jacob Rasch, and myself.

Bottom row: Sam Hambrick, Tori Lahrman, Zach Brandt, and Roxy Ward

Courtesy of Tori Lahrman

Picture of me while on my camel safari in Pushkar, Rajasthan. As you can see, I bartered for my wardrobe. Taken during my time in India through Project GO, July of 2019.

Courtesy of Angelo Di Mondo

Me practicing positive foreign relations for the United States with an enlisted Indian soldier. Taken at a Delhi Train Station, August of 2019.

Courtesy of Angelo Di Mondo

Cadet Zach Brandt (first to the right) and I before the Marksmanship event during the Ranger Challenge competition. Taken in October, 2019.

Courtesy of the Carroll College Military Science Department

My friends Dawson, Will, and I after completing the Murph memorial workout during the "COVID summer" of 2020.

Pictured (from left to right): Dawson Zebarth, myself, and Will Nocé-Sheldon

Courtesy of Will Nocé-Sheldon

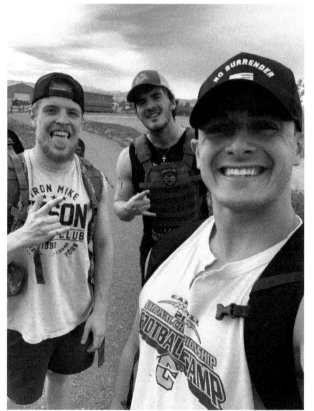

Cadet Trevor Drinville posing with the M249SAW machine gun during Operation Agile Leader (OAL). Taken in August, 2020.

Courtesy of CPT Christopher Clark

Cadets Jacob Rasch, Tori Lahrman, and I between STX lanes at OAL. Taken in August, 2020.

Courtesy of Jacob Rasch

The Class of 2021 before a helicopter ride on a CH-47 Chinook before Spring FTX. Taken one month before commissioning, April of 2021.

Courtesy of the Carroll College Military Science Department

PART II: A Personal History

Chapter 5: Gaze into the Unknown

Before the beginning there was once this end. A time where the friends I knew, the places I drove, the stars I would gaze upon, were one and the same. I had not known anything different for what seemed like a lifetime. I had my team, my brothers, a band of misfits ready to take on the world. Life was consistent in its flow: both predictable and beautiful.

I had a first love that filled up my spirit, she rejuvenated my vitality down to my last parcel of tissue. I had a collection of untouched dreams that were pure-spirited and innocent, ready to be claimed. I had tasted both success and defeat, but felt unshaken in their wake. I was ready for life to change, excited for the mystery, ready to gaze into the unknown.

-

Right before Christmas day of my senior year of high school, my mother and my step-father had temporarily split. I wanted to provide her and the rest of my family a special Christmas. I finally had money to give and I desired to give them a holiday of joy, especially because I was going to be in college the following year.

We finished exchanging gifts, she was pleasantly surprised by how hard her sons worked to give her a meaningful Christmas morning. She pulled me into the kitchen, I was the last one to hear her breaking news. Judging by the quizzical and energized look on her face, I could tell she was nervous. Her brows seemed to flow like the Puget Sound, it seemed so unsettling, and subtle. I had to hear what she had to say. She told me that she was pregnant, this was my stepfather's child. At first, I could not react, I had to scramble inside my brain for a proper response. Then like a sudden ray of sunshine, I was thrilled for her, I could not wait to meet my little sibling. She had known for a few months; I could tell all of this change had taken a toll on her.

A similar moment happened a few years before, right after we moved to Seattle, when my current stepmother found out she was pregnant with my father's child. At the time, I reacted in the exact opposite way, I was angry, flustered, and shaken. Few moments can irritate you in a manner that warrants direct anger towards someone you love. My young conscious could not handle the weight of my life's randomness. Once I heard the news from my mother, I quickly realized my responsibility as a young man only intensified. I had to be joyous for new life and embrace life's curveballs.

Over the next few months, she began to experience increased signs of pregnancy. I felt obligated to assist her anyway possible because she was living by herself. Assistance included groceries (diet Dr. Pepper and pickles were her favorite), quality time, and any other necessary errands that ensured she was physiologically stable and happy. Around this time, I made the decision to pursue a path in the military.

My lifelong dream of becoming a college football player seemed like old news. I wanted a challenge and I knew the military could give it to me.

While I was trying to figure out where to go for school, I began working this job at a grocery store. Bagging, cleaning, and stocking the store were my main responsibilities at my job at Quality Food Centers. I began working hard and saving money for the currently unknown after high school. At this point I was pretty over-weight; I stood at 276 lbs. at my heaviest. At 6'1 with broad shoulders, I was stocky with above average height—*The 'perfect' body structure for the Army.* Years of bad eating habits and training for football got me to this condition.

Once I had googled the Army's standards for height and weight, I was taken aback at how much weight I would have to lose in order to simply qualify. On that computer screen, the Army told me that I would have to lose over 80 lbs. to not be considered overweight. This target weight was incredibly daunting, it seemed impossible. Like any goal worth achieving, I figured I had to start from scratch and give it my best shot.

-

During high school, I had battled with injuries in football for about two years. I was caught up in a routine of getting healthy then being immediately sidelined. I was used to losing all the work I put in, this process was nothing new to me. Just like before, I figured it would be a rise and fall progression towards success. I could not have been more correct, moments of pure joy and insecurity seemed to coincide rapidly.

I started attacking this seemingly lofty goal of joining the Army with small, calculated steps. I wrote it down on a legal notepad, like weekly objectives for me to track my progress and shortcomings. My initial goal-setting was simple and somewhat naive towards my body's exodus. I was not sure if it would work.

My father lived about a quarter of a mile away from my mother's house in Issaquah, Washington. I figured my first runs would be to and from there after work. On my first run I did not make it two blocks before my faced turned cherry red. I thought I was going to pass out and die. Immediately after I could not feel my lungs, legs, or head. I was dizzy, nauseous, and seriously considered quitting. If you know me, you would know that I could not bear to live with myself if I quit. So, I continued this seemingly infinite run of a quarter mile for the next few days.

After about a week I knew I could run a greater distance. I decided to do this same run twice. Again, my heart seemed to be pounding out of my chest, my legs turned to a Jell-O like substance. I repeated this process for another week, finding the urge to increase the mileage yet again. My running continued for about a month until I lost about fifteen pounds, now "running" four miles. I could not believe that I could now complete four miles. If you had asked me a few months before to run that, I would have gone to the refrigerator and washed my goal down my throat. I was not out of the woods; I had a long way to go before I could even qualify for the Army.

-

The routine of school, work, and my runs continued till the end of my senior year. At this point school was on the back burner. I was only concerned with my job, friends, family, and my mother especially. My friends and I could not imagine our near future, being separated from each other soon. We had been through thick and thin, won two state titles for football, and shared countless mornings, afternoons, and nights together. We constantly debated what would or could happen to each of us. We were practically counting the days when it would be over, it seemed to be the elephant in the room when we hung out those final few months.

The military seemed so foreign to my life right before college. Once graduation commenced, I was not excited about the accomplishments of my friends, peers, and myself. All of it felt almost childish and unnecessary. I wanted something new in my life, a sense of purpose. I required goal to go after and achieve. While to many this may sound crazy, I knew the military could help me discover myself. The Army appealed to me because of the challenge it required. I saw how my conscious embedded itself in the mirror; I wanted to reshape how I held my head.

-

Soon enough summer arrived, beginning my new job at this local lumber yard. I opened the lot by cleaning, filling customers' trucks with orders, and organizing inventory. This job sucked the life out of me every day. Additionally, it gave me another reason to pursue the military and my education. I got to know the customers and my fellow employees, I wanted something greater out of my life. My opinion was slightly arrogant but I interpreted it to be necessary for my long-term development.

I decided to go to Carroll almost off of a whim. After working here I knew it was the right choice. These early summer days seemed incredibly long and dry. I continued to visit my mother, especially as her pregnancy progressed and my runs became longer and more difficult.

My baby sister was born in June of that summer, giving me a connection that I had never experienced before. Siena is someone I had a role in taking care of despite having limited responsibilities. I immediately fell in love; it warmed my heart to hold and care for her. I witnessed some of her first words, steps, and cries. I came over almost every day to be with her and help however I could. Just as she was taking her first steps, I was taking mine. I had to learn how to walk again. I was taking the same small steps forward, learning along the way like her. Within the week of her arrival, it dawned on me to take another leap of courage in a different area of my life.

-

I had met this foreign exchange student about a year before my mother told me about her pregnancy. We met through a friend of mine, quickly becoming close friends. She asked me to this dance (like Sadie Hawkins, TOLO, etc.). The night of the dance I discovered that I *like-liked* this girl. We got closer with one another but the fact remained that she was leaving in only a few months. I could not make a proper move to ask her out because of the duration on her exchange program. The end date agitated me but remained true no matter what my aspirations had to say.

Prom arrived soon after and I decided to ask her to be my date since there are no Prom or high school dances of any kind in Germany. On Prom night, I fell under the same spell as countless before have, knowing that I was in love with her. I had never been that open and vulnerable to another person before, everything with her meant the world to me. I was extremely downtrodden for the end of the night together and her too-soon departure.

We continued to talk once she arrived home, progressing until the summer before college. That June, around the same time as the birth of my baby sister, I was possessed by this urge to visit her in Germany. I needed to illustrate how much I cared for her. Before I went, I continued working at the lumber yard, picking up two more landscaping jobs to have enough money for college and my trip. While many of my classmates were enjoying their summer after high school, I was employed and running non-stop. It took every ounce of energy and focus I had to save up enough money to make this journey happen.

Once I purchased my plane ticket, emotions of all kinds flooded my insides. I was taking a step I knew to be necessary, something I had to do. It was an attempted resolving of an unfulfilled urge deep in my insides. A young man possesses these emotions, whether right or wrong they are pure and beautiful in their innocence. We have this color attached to us as young people that we somehow lose as we become adults. Few choices like this exist, regardless its process is an elevation of the spirit, a transcendence towards the trust forms of the world. Needless to say, I now interpret mine to be a bold choice made out of ignorance. I was uncomfortable towards the unknown, fearful of the negative. My life seemed to hang on a single thread: my first love, my finances, my physical training... I was barely scraping by and was not sure if I could handle a single failure.

-

Once I arrived in Germany, a blanket of euphoria covered me, I was in awe of this new country that I journeyed to on my own. *I had paid for this completely, this was my idea, I made this happen!* It was unreal to me; I craved every moment of it. I got off the plane and quickly got on a train to Bonn, a suburb of Cologne, and reunited with her.

Just as I had imagined, she took my breath away upon seeing her again. I knew how much I missed her; I did not want to let go once we reunited. In the next few days her, her family, and I traveled the western part of Germany together. We traveled all across the Rhine, seeing cities, studying castles, and touring other historic sites. I never had the right moment to tell her I loved her but I hardly cared. I was there with her, unsure if I would ever see her again. It all had to be worth it.

The last night in Bonn quickly fell unto my lap, I was departing the train for Berlin the next morning. I could not sleep and was consumed by nervousness. I had never been in a state like this in my entire life. I was awake by sunrise, packing and preparing for my leave. Her family and I got in the car and drove thirty minutes to Cologne to the train station. My stomach seemed to roll with the tires of the car, my mind was going at the speed of the autobahn. I subtly began to sweat and shake, my mind either wanted to punch a wall or hide in a corner. I found myself dumbfounded on the proper manner to act in this situation, my awareness to my condition only heightened my body's symptoms.

We finally reached the train station and it eased my blood pressure to walk despite treading towards our goodbye. My train stop seemed extra hectic that morning. Looking up, I saw there were twenty minutes before I had to make my move. I was frantically chewing my gum, vastly uncomfortable with a semi-normal expression on my face. Twenty minutes was infinite but extremely fast. The clock's ticks seemed to fly right over my head, having no consideration for what my psyche could handle—*I took a leap and went for it.*

A flash whisps by, I hear the sound of the train eventually headed towards Berlin. I thought to myself, "Six hours is a long time if this does not go well." The train seems to know my plans, slithering to a halt. Steam exits the doors like smoke as they slide open, alike to a witch's cauldron. I begin my goodbyes and conclude once I step in front of her. I decided in advance that no matter who was there I was going to make my move and *kiss* her. It took every muscle in my body to go for it. As I inch forward, she moves to my left side, avoiding my love life's salvation.

No.
What?
Why??

I exit to the train doors, daring not to look back, unsure of what I did wrong or what just occurred. The doors close and I am on my way to Berlin. The past moments kept rewinding and playing in my brain's movie theater. *It never stopped the whole train ride to Berlin.* Unbearable to watch, it made my face blue once I saw it on the big screen. It wiped away all of my feeling, the perfect end to a backwards romance film. Anticlimactic in its ending, it left me extremely solitary by its plot twist. Everything I had done until that moment seemed washed away, my old self got soaked in bleach. I never saw her again since that morning.

-

About two weeks after I got back from Germany, I left for Montana to begin college. Upon return, I realized I could never feel the same as before. I had aged ten years since I left home. I felt older and extremely more confused about the past few months. I looked onward to my first semester of college, completely unsure of what ROTC was going to be and how I would handle myself as a college student.

The effects of the past year seeped in. I was more or less the same for a few months after until it all hit me suddenly, sending me to the floor. Crashing to an unknown pit where I knew I had changed for the worse, I was distraught and brittle at the bone. I lost a lot of self-confidence after that moment. I initially retreated, further exacerbating the issues that rose to my surface. I barely had enough money to pay for school and no guaranteed scholarship in the ROTC program. I was going in blind, unsure if I was going to be able to pull it together. I needed a way to pay for school, I wanted to serve in the military, and I needed to find myself again.

-

Humanity's acquisition of knowledge is attainable through the chasm of personal experience. The majority of young individuals' intellectual discoveries are often the fruits of mistakes, a mechanism of receiving wisdom. Only in such tension is mankind able to garner any parcel of self-actualization. Humanity is guided, swayed, and defined by our emotions. Anger, happiness, fear, confidence, failure, and success are the building blocks to our soul's fire.

Human life is the procedural maintenance of the soul's fire. Sometimes you have to leave the campsite to gather more wood while the fire gets cold. You come back and get goosebumps because it is not as warm as you once remember. You miss that comfort and its warmth, but you needed to gather more timber right? It is necessary and crucial to do so for the fire's survival. Failure is the same thing. Failure will smack you in the face but it often gives you the best advice moving forward. Don't be discouraged, push through the pain.

Chapter 6: The Void

When we discuss what limited me—the *once seen* and the *present*, we must discuss my manner of approach. I was marred with insecurities and lacked the belief in myself to achieve something great. I wanted to settle and enjoy my life, reducing the number of challenges I had to face on a daily basis. My thought process led to many long days and nights, confused, fearful, and unable to rest peacefully.

I would stare at the ceiling and try to guess the time, periodically checking my watch to see if I was correct. My routine would continue until the alarm clock would ring, still awake from the night before. Some mornings I would have PT and I felt like I was giving it my all regardless of the workout. I had so much stress and such little rest, college sucked my vitality dry. Your mind can only handle so much turbulence and unease, my life began to tear me down dramatically.

I lacked a great amount of direction and purpose. I started aimlessly trying to find methods to help me sleep and navigate my life. Some nights I would sit on the floor alone, in the hallways of Guadalupe hall, writing deep into the night. *Why?* I honestly have no idea.

My night-writing continued until I had about three chapters on my laptop. I asked myself what I was going to do with the work on my desk. *Should I continue? Should this be a phase? What do I make of this humble amount of work?* I decided I wanted to challenge myself greatly, I aimed to do something I never thought I could do: write a book. I told very few people and I doubt any believed me. I wanted to keep this secret to many and put in my work silently. *Maybe the answers were in the words, maybe there was something more in what I had to say about myself.*

-

I just want to be free, free of constraints on my life, unrestricted in the dreams I yearn to achieve. I miss this feeling and its way of curing my days —the days outside of my own prison. It is fulfillment in the little things through the melodies and colors of the world. It reaches down inside, pulling me out of the deep darkness. I want to breathe and sleep peacefully. I know I can take the difficult path but I do not feel equipped to do so.

The life I am living is unfulfilling and I am scared of easy things. I used to welcome a crowd, now I cannot be unseen by the multitudes. Any attention makes me uncomfortable. My heart is still invisible, I cannot be heard while I scream, my voice lacks its normal tune.

I fear this haven to evil's sanctity. One that echoes the sounds of the consistent dead beats of a day. I cannot live sitting here alone, shaken by every aspect of experience. I want to go away, far away, with my imagination. I dream of hearing the smooth ocean tide crash against the sand. My heaven is vibrant with inner peace, completely opposite to the abomination I see myself as. Life has told me that my heaven is no longer attainable.

The pain I hold unto is nothing anyone can understand. My past creeps on me, the present makes me shiver like a winter's storm, and the future makes me want to cower. I sit here beside myself, wondering why my life has happened and why I still stand today.

-

I began to redirect my energies once I started to write. I had to unravel myself, like a giant knot, and search for my source of anguish. I initially thought the perspectives and praises of others would help the heaviness I felt inside. Such attempts only aid temporarily, it is a quick fix to your life's disease, unfulfilling in every manner possible. I wanted to be cool, funny, a leader, selfless, and honestly, glorified. My ego blew up like a hot balloon, eventually popping, releasing a loud pop with steam, absent of all substance.

My friends could relate. Class, homework, PT, Lab, finances, girls...My schedule was pointless, monotonous, a waste of my time. I wanted to get a free pass to all the rewards I did not deserve. Mainly, I wanted to feel good about myself because I had not in a long time. I routinely made excuses for myself. My friends and classmates related heavily.

When asked about his first two years at Carroll, Senior Cadet Trevor Drinville recalls, "I was unmotivated, unsure of where I was headed in life. I discovered I became utterly confused about what I was doing and why I was doing it."[21] Certain nights we would sit on a random park bench because none of us wanted to wake up for the following morning. The next day was too difficult to bear, we could not handle it, at least we had each other.

For better or worse, a bond began to form, over a spite of how we lived and tasted the world. We enjoyed being idiots because a parcel of us wanted the world to feel how we did. Grades, attendance, performance in all respects, began to slip. Out of my friends and I, I knew I restricted my potential the most. I had earned a scholarship and an opportunity for a quality education but was still ungrateful. I did not care how I did, none of it mattered. I had no concept of what I wanted, so why try? We finished the schoolyear unsure of what to do next. I debated transferring, enlisting, or simply quitting over my first year and a half at Carroll.

I hated everything about my life. I wanted to change it and lacked the courage to do so. In my mind opting out was much easier to comprehend and articulate. It made sense to quit on paper, it was the path of least resistance. I sought comfort in all parts of life but the greater comfort I gave myself, the worse I became. I formed bad habits, especially bad self-talk. I always had an ongoing negative dialogue playing in my head. I would put my peers and idols on a pedestal—*How could I do that? I can't do that. I am fat, lazy, and unintelligent. I am not talented like them.*

I put my talents and vigor in a box, locked it tight, and hid it deep in the inner reaches of my heart. I was afraid of getting hurt, rejected, and frowned upon. I created this void for myself: a selfish, self-induced prism of jealousy, ignorance, and pain. I would not be stating this if it was not completely honest and authentic. Individuals of all types need to hear this, whether they have experienced this or not. I am comfortable describing this experience because I have come to terms with my flaws and internal issues. Your transgressions should be worn upon your sleeve because *they are who you are*, whether you admit it or not. I had to learn the hard way, listen to what I have to say.

-

The summer after my freshman year I came back home and was happy to be back at a place that was normal. I had my old friends, my old restaurants, and my family. I got a job at a meat company in downtown Seattle, near SODO, at a company called Corfini Gourmet Incorporated. I was initially hired as a social media intern but due to a grave need for workers in the workhouse, I switched my job title and began working as a warehouse worker.

I had tremendous respect for the manager of the warehouse, Todd. His leadership and sacrifice for the company was in my opinion greatly under appreciated. Todd had an incredible presence about him, always early, doing more than what was asked of him every day. He took the time to get to know his employees and the company's customers. He was an engaging manager, filling in areas where his superiors and subordinates failed or neglected.

Contrary to Todd, I also dealt with very toxic management, managers who would make fellow employees cry, flare at the nostrils, and quit. I saw how subordinates reacted to these two types of managers. The toxic leaders and employees of this company lacked the presence, empathy, and selflessness that Todd exemplified. I found myself at odds as a young intern, unsure of how to handle different types of employees, customers, and my own fluctuating emotions.

I decided I would just do my job—clean, sweep, and fill out orders. One of my main roles was scraping the ice out of this meat freezer. Every day, six times a day, I would scrape the ice off of the frozen fish, beef, and pork boxes. The ice would corrode the freezer, etch itself unto the walls, and unite to the coating of the boxes. Here, I began to sink deeper into my hole—*Why am I working here when my friends do not know how hard my life is?*

I felt bad for myself routinely. Amidst my increasingly negative outlook, Todd's upcoming weeks were much worse than mine, he was forced to fire all but one of our night crew workers. I saw him come in for two weeks straight, red eyed, crushing two 32 oz. Monsters a day, occasionally falling asleep on his keyboard from exhaustion.

As a manager, he was the only man working nights. I stood back and watched him wither away in the warehouse. I was uncomfortable with my job but I had no idea how Todd could keep up daily. I was unsure of what to do. *Should I let him keep working this way? I hate my job already; I do not want to work nights. Why should I? That would make my hard job even harder.*

My negative self-talk multiplied, expanding daily. I hit a breaking point and became sick with how I was acting. I asked my manager to switch to the night shift to help Todd. My shift began at 11 pm and ended at 8 am six days a week. My brother would drop me off deep in the heart of Seattle during the night. My shift was followed by an hour and a half bus ride home the next morning. *Cold* was one word to describe that work. By shift's end I wanted to burn down that god forsaken meat freezer. My back would ache every night at work and every morning when trying to sleep. *How could I live like this?* I seriously considered quitting but kept treading forward anyway.

Eventually I began to callous, getting more determined by the day. I would clean, scrape the freezer, fill out orders, load the trucks, check our inventory, and clean the trucks upon return. I started to get skilled at my job, craving work because I enjoyed the challenge it warranted. The two-mile walks to the bus stop on shift's end did not seem dreadful anymore. I had an inner peace towards my difficult routine. I relished in my labor because subconsciously I knew that I desperately needed this experience.

-

That summer I took the second step I needed to find myself. I did something difficult, a job most people would quit. I stuck with it till the end and it gave me a humble outlook on myself. It made me tolerate a greater amount of difficulty and expect less from others. I desired more out of my life because I slowly began to understand the harshness of the real world. While I have and am living more comfortably than many, I knew it was not an easy task to complete. I stretched my comfort zone significantly during this time. I began to believe that I was much more perseverant than I previously conceived.

I came back to Carroll that Fall rejuvenated yet running into the same internal roadblocks I had encountered my freshman year. By semester's end, daily tasks made me nauseous; I could hardly bear to be around my friends because of how self-conscious I became. It was the most difficult and longstanding period of my life. For a year and a half, I felt alone facing my problems and internal dilemmas.

I was by myself for the first time, on my own accord, facing the difficulties in front of me. It all wore me down. My first year and a half of college was the wake-up call I needed to change my life's trajectory.

When asked about my development over the past four years, Cadet Jacob Rasch said, "Nate learned confidence despite no prior experience, becoming a much more confident decision maker overall. Performance and career are now priorities for him and he consciously avoided the college scene. He has identified what he wants and is going after it with everything he has. I respect the hell out of that."[21] Without the nature of my arrival at Carroll, I do not believe I would have changed positively over my duration in Helena.

I had to overcome the shortcomings I made at this point to instill proper motivation and expectation of how I needed to work. Life was not going to hand me what I wanted. It became crystal clear that I had to work consciously towards my objectives and dreams.

The following year of 2019, I committed myself in making it the best year of my life. I wanted to lay it all out on the table, live life without regret, and achieve the goals I set out for myself that year. I woke up on New Year's Day with a fresh intent, a fresh attitude, and a perspective tailored to embracing the entirety of life. Compared to a year and a half ago, my outlook on failure was the exact opposite. I had to embrace the unknowns of my future because whether good or bad, they made me better than before. My aspirations required focused, timely actions to ensure success. The only way through life's mess is forward, allow it to transform you in your process of achieving self-actualization.

Chapter 7: A Second Chance

Of the follies and pitfalls that riddled the first half of my time at Carroll College, I knew that this was the time to change. I wrote my goals out, in every aspect of my life, in a detailed and calculated manner. My plans consisted of timely constraints, allergic to internal blockades from fear. I needed to improve *physically*, I desired to evolve *personally*, and I organized an outlook focused on *self-development* for every waking day.

At the inception of the winter semester of 2019, I moved into a small closet like space in the far corner of Saint Charles. The room overlooked the western side of the school and the valley beyond. My room illustrated my work process in its infancy—isolated, difficult, and humble in its beginnings. As my first night came to a close, I knew this year would be different than all previous. I still did not know how to properly get there.

-

I made it the primary goal of each day to challenge myself. I studied more, I exercised more, I read more, and I wrote more. I started checking my email more frequently, paying greater attention in class. It paid off right away as I found myself more engaged in the activities I was involved in, finding greater enjoyment in what I was doing. My plans and products became detailed, I wanted to display passion in my responsibilities.

The winter hit pretty hard that year, regular snowpack, cold temperatures, and reduced motivation were heavily prevalent throughout. I studied, would run or go to the gym, shower, continue writing my book, and read right before I went to bed. Nervousness was still a cloud over my head but I now had tremendous confidence to conquer my daily fears. My sleep schedule was still riddled with inconsistency. I had the outlook of if I cannot sleep, I would be productive instead. Cold nightly runs, writing, and constantly learning were my remedies for this issue.

As the semester progressed, I started seeing changes in my athletic and academic performance. *Focus* was one way to describe this period. I had a second chance at reclaiming what was rightfully mine and I was taking full advantage in any possible manner. Just as my hopes were starting to dim, I was given notice of an opportunity to study abroad in Delhi, India.

Through Project GO, I was able to acquire 8 credits in the language of Urdu while living in India for about two months. Urdu is primarily spoken in the northern region of India in Jammu and Kashmir, the eastern side of Pakistan, and the southern region of Afghanistan. The vocabulaury is almost identical to Hindi, featuring an Arabic script and terms and letters from the Arabic alphabet (primarily in the context of Islam).

While planning my trip to India, I continued training for my record APFT fitness test at the end of the semester and my classes. My book was turning out well, I needed about four chapters done by the year's end, and was planning on revising my entire summer. Overall life seemed to be showing meaningful improvements but I still felt distant towards my classmates and friends. Being isolated cut me off from continuing close-relationships with many in my general proximity. I read the world differently because of what I had experienced. Whereas before I was jealous and even bitter, now I was alone because I was working on my goals in solitude. This outlook had eventual benefits but was difficult to manage at first.

-

A lot of my classmates in ROTC earned opportunities that they rightfully deserved because they performed better when I slacked in my obligations. I was playing catchup for at least a semester, knowing I had to prove myself over an extended period of time to get additional training opportunities. Regularly it is not the judge of performance in the short-term but endurance over time that dictates being granted blessings. ROTC is an optimal example of this, as cadets are usually rewarded for their hard work in the program as a cadet. Training opportunities include Army schools, programs abroad, and access to certain training events.

One's attendance on these events or programs usually correctly reflects their dedication overall. I sound odd hearing myself contemplate my feelings my first two years. Upon recollection I was overcame with pride and selfishness during my initial period at Carroll. I wanted all of the awards, recognition, and anything to "look good." I never achieved my goals because I was not focused properly, not delivering my end of the bargain. I stopped caring about this "cadet prestige" because I was not happy with my life. I held unto internal and external issues in my life.

My energy deviated from pursuing the meaningless acceptance from my peers, cadre, and family towards wholesome fulfillment encompassing my life. Who cares about those stupid awards? Who cares about the schools you attend? You make your own opportunities, focus on what you can control daily. 2019 was the year about *me* and how I could respond to adversity. In order to achieve self-actualization, you have to put in the work. This became my new perspective. Ignorance and lack of self-responsibility actually helped me address what my problems were as a student, cadet, and individual.

-

I was regularly sorting out what I wanted to do for my future in the Army. I still had no idea and felt I had a rough sketch for my next few years. The Judge Advocate General Corps (JAG) was my solid, tentative plan. Pursuing law school was an educational goal worth pursuing because I deemed it necessary for my personal development. I knew that if I could write, debate, and think critically I could achieve greater long-term success in my professional career. The Army's service requirements under my contract conflicts with my dream of attending law school because JAG did not fulfill what I desired out of my service.

Deep-down, I desired to lead people directly, especially in a setting like the battlefield. Early on, I felt like a child in the Boy Scouts running around at Lab and FTX, asking myself, "This is the Army?". I debated enlisting several times because of this lack of satisfaction. Such tension bothered me constantly in 2018 and 2019.

I put all my concerns and anxiety in my back-pocket. *Aspirations need time to resolve themselves.* I redirected this energy towards my school assignments and dreams on the near horizon. My college education and my involvement in the ROTC program evolved into a newfound source of pride once I displayed passion through my contributions. My educational routine continued day by day and night by night. I was desperate for fresh energy to captivate my days. I inched closer to my goals knowing there was positive change right in front of my face.

-

By semester's end I was near the finish line, seeing the need to finish strongly in school and in ROTC. My confidence in leadership labs and FTXs improved greatly during this period. My focus was paying off, resulting in more confident decision making and the acquisition of necessary leadership experience.

When asked about my leadership development, former Cadet and current 2nd Leiutanent Parker Perry said, "I think the result of Nate's first ruck march says it all. He got huge blisters that covered the entirety of his feet's soles during his first week I believe. The transition from that morning to him leading ranger challenge, commissioning as an active-duty infantry officer speaks for itself...he showed up, got his feet ripped to shreds, and his lunch taken. Now, he's helping lead the pack, making an impact. He truly cares about the program and its members."[18]

Throughout the semester, the date of my record APFT test loomed on my calendar. The test itself was not a big deal, it was what it symbolized to me. Considering my development so far, I had to prove to myself that I could max out the test. I was the heaviest cadet in the program at the time, at about 232 lbs. The heaviest cadet is not expected to have a great PT score, much less maxing it. I wanted a perfect score because I knew that it was *possible*.

The night of the test I was more than ready. I could barely sleep and woke up the next morning ecstatic for that morning. Between events I was silent, isolating myself. All the buildup over the semester summoned all of my focus, giving me an ambitious headache. First came pushups...*done*. Next came sit-ups...*check*. Finally, came the two-mile run, my worst event on most APFT tests.

I started off with a solid pace but was slowing down near the halfway portion of the run. Off in the distance I heard the time, realizing I had a minute left to finish. Near the end, I sprinted with nothing held back to the finish line to make the cut-off time of thirteen minutes. Cadet Daniel Guthrie saw me run at the finish line, describing the final portion of the run: "CPT Thompson started counting off at 12:50, about fifty yards out. Nate was drooling to make the necessary time. All of the previous finishers were saying obscenities to motivate him to move quicker to the finish line. I have never seen someone move so fast, especially being a bigger guy. CPT Thompson finished counting right at his finish at a time of 13 minutes flat."[23]

I could not believe that I achieved it. A 316 APFT score meant I disproved others' expectations of how I could physically perform. My score was meaningful because of where I started: *those quarter mile runs to my mom's apartment.* My miniscule triumph told others that even if you are not physical ready upon arrival at this ROTC program, you have an ability to develop your physical state. I was proud of this score only because of the process I had to undertake to achieve it. *This was a small step in the right direction...*

About a week later, I decided to attend the Spartan BEAST run in Bigfork, Montana. The race consisted of 30+ obstacles on a fourteen-mile path located in the foothills behind Bigfork. I had never run that distance before nor gone over obstacles featured at the Spartan race. I drove to the race with Cadet Rasch, neither of us feeling prepared whatsoever. We were both in good physical shape but did not train properly for the nature of this race. My time did not matter to me, I just wanted to finish. Finishing meant that all the training was paying off.

We began the race the next morning and I felt strong for the first few miles. The obstacles were easier than expected, I was confident in my ability to finish with a great time despite my initial concerns. I got soaked in ice-laden ponds, crawled through mud, climbed and swinged, and tested my overall cardiovascular endurance continuously throughout.

About mile nine I began to cramp heavily in my calves. Already worn down by the previous portion, my legs were nearly drained of energy. It took sheer will to get through the next few miles. *Will* was all I had (I literally did not pack water or food) for the remainder of this race. At mile twelve I was feeling more dead than alive, literally and metaphorically soaking in misery. Following was the first true runner's high I have ever experienced.

Like a summer's dream, I was jovial in my suffering. Clarity pervaded my mind, fueling my muscles, and my thirst to finish. I had three miles left. The finish line seemed so far away but I had no necessity for the race to end. The day's ongoing process stitched my wounds and fears shut. I arrived at the race's end amidst my day-dreaming rather faster than expected. Bliss filled my muscles and bones, strength returned from where it was absent. I climbed over the final obstacle and jumped with triumph at the finish line (I beat Cadet Rasch). Summer was here, India was the next objective of 2019.

-

Before my arrival in New Delhi, I spent a week in Hong Kong traveling, hiking, and sightseeing. A new world was right in front of me ready for my spirit's claim. I met men and women of all backgrounds, careers, and interests. The food was packed with flavor, every meal changed my outlook on what was culinarily possible. Especially the bowl of boiled frog I accidentally ordered because I could not read the menu. *No, it did not taste good.* My time was brief but incredibly beneficial.

My final day's plans were derailed by the riots and protests on Hong Kong Island. Literally right outside of my hostel on Hennessy road, I saw people adorned in pure white, creating change in the country they inhabited. I witnessed the beatings of protestors about twenty feet from where I stood. I heard their agony and cries while the Chinese Riot Control crushed the chosen few nearly to a pulp.

As I left for the airport, I saw the riot's preceding events and its conclusion on social media and on television. Tear gas, blood, and armed policemen painted the digital screens and worldwide newsfeeds. Witnessing this firsthand affected me in an unidentifiable way in the moment. It dawned on me during the long airplane ride to Delhi: while America nor myself could help everyone in need, I wanted to try the best I could during the course of my life. People near and far away from you suffer. It is your responsibility to help individuals of this world in any manner possible, whether in miniscule or seemingly ambitious ways.

-

India was hot like its summer sun, it was rejuvenating and draining at the same time. This country's character grasped an ancient and cutting edge: the duality of global poverty and the world's finest technology. I was in awe of the business buildings, malls, and medical care. On the contrary, I was agast by the slums, pollution, and the state of this nation's children.

My roommate and I lived two houses away from a slum. While we were confined to a one-room rooftop space, we overlooked a small building housing twelve people. About half of its walls were broken in, literally hanging by threads. The family's privacy was adorned by a humble veil of clothes and cloths. The yard consisted of three layers of heavily compressed trash, in colors and brands of all sources. It was eye-opening to be in such proximity to poverty firsthand. The struggles of India's people riddled the city streets and sidewalks while I was studying on a whim, a lucky educational opportunity.

Despite the gut-check I got from my travels so far, I loved every aspect of my journey. My program and I were able to see the religious and historical sites of Delhi and central India. Notable examples include the Taj Mahal, Gurudwara Sahib, the Red Fort, the Amber Palace, the Wind Palace, the Monkey Temple, a Camel Safari, and a splendid afternoon riding and feeding Elephants. When we were not sight-seeing we were usually in school, learning Urdu about eight hours each weekday. After school Angelo and I would study at a local cafe, Blue Tokai or exercise at a gym near our home. We frequently traveled the subway, at least an hour ride there and back for any destination. When we woke up adventurous, we took tuk-tuks and bartered with the local drivers over our taxi fees.

The most memorable journey we experienced was from Delhi to the Taj Mahal in Agra. On our Uber ride, our driver would stop every ten minutes, peeing or taking a smoke break. Our driver actually tried to pick up his friends and relatives three times in a crammed car, running out of gas twice during the drive. During the first twenty minutes, he spit on my roommate while getting rid of a tobacco product in his mouth.

Furthermore, he refused to turn on the air-conditioning in 110-degree heat because it was not incorporated into our cab-fare. The five-hour drive turned to twelve hours, taking the course of the day. While the Taj Mahal was as beautiful and intricate as the history books say, we did not really care upon arrival. By the end of the day, we just wanted to go to bed, wondering how the hell *today* just happened.

-

Bazaars were adorned with knockoff Nike, Gucci, Dickies, and Prada. After a few weeks, I got rather good at haggling getting the best value prices on food, clothes, or other necessary items. Funny enough, locals wanted to take a selfie with me in public spaces. I am not sure as to the exact reason why but everywhere we traveled to, someone wanted a selfie with either I or my friends.

A great example of this was during our stay in Pushkar, Rajasthan where a child was in charge of the hotel we stayed in. His hotel was incredibly disgusting. Rat poop was scattered across the rooms, sponge-buckets replaced showers, and spiders and insects of all sorts were prevalent throughout the beds. The child hotel manager hated us because we complained about the conditions of the rooms. Right after we angrily requested a refund, he requested a selfie with us with a smile on his face. *We agreed to comply.*

My friends and classmates in the Project GO program were mainly cadets of all military branches from schools across the country. Universities such as Notre Dame, Yale, Brigham Young, North Carolina State, and Rutgers were examples. We were split into two language programs: Urdu and Hindi. Both languages had seperate campuses for learning. The Urdu program was located at the Zabaan learning academy, in the Visant Vihar neighborhood of New Delhi. My friends and I usually spent the weekends traveling to sites nearby. Lunch breaks during school meant touring the local marketplaces for new foods and stores.

The food was incredibly diverse and tasteful in India. I was able to try many foods of the region, often unsure of what I was getting myself into. Notable examples include Afghani, Gujrati, Punjabi, Benghali, and Kashmeri food. My diet was mainly vegetarian, comprised of rice, paneer, daal, and naan almost every meal. Chicken and pork were not commonly served, most protein came from the cream in your chai or through paneer (goat cheese). Most restaraunts serving meat were in North Delhi near the Jama Masjid mosque. North Delhi was about a two-hour subway ride from our home so we did not journey there often.

About halfway through the program, the joys of the summer began to fade as the new school year rose to the forefront of my mind. I wanted to compete in our ranger challenge team upon arrival back at Carroll. Similar to the previous semester, I adopted a strict physical routine and vegetarian diet to lose weight and regain optimal physical performance. I regularly did a run near my townhouse in Delhi in a local park. It was about a half mile on a hardly paved sidewalk. My runs required watching for nearby cricket players as they hit balls in the tree branches above my head.

As Urdu's curriculum increasingly challenged myself so too did my runs. Monsoon season randomly and quickly filled Delhi's foundations to the brim. The dry, 114-degree air became a humid, soaking downpour of 105 degrees. Most nights I continued my runs despite half the roads being flooded. I found great enjoyment in struggling in the storms and its heat, seeing it as a proving-grounds for the months and years ahead.

My roommate, Angelo became a great source of inspiration for me as I voiced my recent experiences. He was the first one to completely believe in me, telling me that I could pursue my dreams in the Army and in life. Around this time, I expressed my thoughts to join the Infantry. Angelo affirmed my humble confidence within myself. He was a second source of advice, a sense of unfound sensibility that I desperately needed.

This was a giant step for me, the impossibilities of achieving my inner callings seemed to shrink exponentially. My ambitions did not seem as crazy, rash, or ignorant. Life brought me here somehow, I was being prepared throughout my existence. My change in perspective shifted my professional aspirations, heightening my intensity in studying and physical training. I imagine myself today if I chose to give up then, especially if I knew what I was truly capable of.

I ended my time in Delhi a much more resilient, ambitious, and confident individual. I was sad to say goodbye to my friends and host family. Maturity was required to endure India and the difficulties of learning a foreign language and society. I was thankful and forever changed by this experience abroad. India has been and always will be a place of victory, defeat, intellectual pursuit, and a site for furthering spiritual understanding. Just as every man and woman have left their mark on this country, I felt I had left mine. The only part that shocked me was how much of an impression it left on me.

-

My classmates had opportunities over this summer for abroad trips as well. Three of Saints Company's cadets went on CULP missions in Chile, Senegal, and Malawi. When asked if CULP adjusted her opinion on the United States abroad, Cadet Tori Lahrman said this about Senegal, "CULP is a crucial experience for cadets because character is revealed in foreign places, especially when interacting with people of a different background from you."[24]

In addition to Senegal, Cadet Lahrman attended a Biodiversity class in Peru that same year. In Peru the program required conducting water research and animal research. Also, students had to interact with cultures on the Amazon not exposed to mass media. When asked about the differences between the trips, she said, "Senegal was a leadership mission, while Peru was much more educational. Both trips required me to not know anyone before-hand. I was going in blind to a new group of individuals and had to conduct research or perform military tasks with them. Both were challenging and rewarding experiences."[24]

Furthermore, Cadet Brandt attended Jungle School in Oahu, Hawaii around the same time as my arrival in New Delhi. When asked about the impact of this training experience, Cadet Brandt said, "I liked it a lot. It is one of those things that gives you a little pride because there are few cadets who have gone there and completed it. I think the time I had in Oahu provided great instruction and training to what an Army school is truly like."[16] Moreover, Cadet Brandt outlines how to be successful at Jungle School: "...take full advantage of free time, take concise notes, and form positive connections upon meeting your squad mates."[16]

-

At summer's end I was excited to hear my friends' experiences while traveling and training. I looked forward to sharing about my time in Delhi and comparing it with my peers and friends' experiences. One beneficial aspect of ROTC is shared experiences. As stated earlier, many of my fellow cadets became my best friends during college. While our experiences, perspectives, and personalities may differ, often there are commonalities shared across individuals. Upon further examination, every facet of life can provide shared mutual understanding. Shared experiences richen your relationships with the individuals you train, compete, and work with.

Our perspectives are not similar to most college students. Most young men and women cannot discuss experiences like Project GO, CULP, or Jungle School. You can take full advantage while attending these strenuous experiences like the four of us did. On the other hand, you can relax and let life take full advantage of you. If you want something deeper, a valuable and more meaningful life, the choice is yours.

-

Fall semester arrived soon enough and I was tasked with training and competing with our ranger challenge team. Being named captain by our Battalion commander meant the world to me. I required vast improvement to be an effective leader and team member of a successful team. I quickly developed a strenuous training plan, aiming for an innovative style, varying from years past.

We trained by rucking, ruck-sprints, long distance runs, heavy weightlifting, swimming, and HIIT circuits. This mixture of short term and long-term cardio, strength training, and focused muscle development differentiated itself from the previous training methods utilized by our ranger challenge team. In the past, training was composed of a simple plan: sprints, rucking, abdominal exercises and distance runs.

The University of Montana's ranger challenge team has always been competitive and successful, winning the first portion of the competition the previous year. I knew that for someone with no previous experience in this competition, I could only lead a successful team by training its members in an inventive manner. Cadets Parker Perry, Jacob Rasch, Zach Brandt, Trevor Drinville, and myself were the main individuals training during our PT sessions in the Fall of 2019.

Our most notable workout was a ruck with a minimum weight of 60 lbs. up the powerline trail at Mount Helena. Later that afternoon at Fort Harrison, we had to practice shooting and go through iterations on the obstacle course with the University of Montana's portion of the team. This training day was structured in this manner to properly assess the physical readiness and overall unit cohesion. In October, Cadet Brandt and I competed with the University of Montana in Cheney, Washington (Eastern Washington University) at the Ranger Challenge Competition.

My first event I struggled heavily. Our team first had to do the Commander's Challenge at the beginning of the competition. The Commander's Challenge entailed scaling a rock-climbing wall, obstacle course run, and the sprint-drag-carry, timed as overall as a team. I failed the rock-climbing wall, slipping every step and every attempt up it. My forearms were already numb from the cold and I developed immense strain while climbing. I did sub-par on the obstacle course but finished the spring-drag-carry strongly.

The competition beat me early on and I almost caught myself getting back into my head. *You are not good enough. You should not be here. You can't do this.* I had to quell these fears and anxieties rapidly in order for the team to succeed throughout the competition.

I quicky responded from my first event, setting the pace for the ruck run and the pontoon race for the second event. We smoked every other team in all physical events. Cadet Ochoa and I were dictating the pace from the front throughout the competition. Our success meant a lot to me because I was the first step, the guy at the start of the pack, moving us forward.

I did not care about the competition itself; I craved the strain it placed on my motivation. Ranger Challenge was a test of what was possible for me as an individual. The goal of winning was not why I competed. Rather, it was the process of becoming, developing, and overcoming my life's fears at the time.

I told myself early on in college that I could never compete on that team. Now I was there, competing. I had to overcome this hurdle by experiencing it, even if I failed in certain respects. People often focus on achieving the end-state, the finish line. Really, we should be focused on the execution or the race itself instead.

-

We killed every physical event. Our team was young, competitive, and rich with vigor. We finished two seconds slower than the University of Gonzaga in the final event, the twelve-mile ruck race. Our team ended up losing by two points, achieving second place. I was slightly disappointed in the results but told myself that I had earned my spot and was a positive contribution to the team. I was grateful for how I personally stepped up my performance during the course of the competition. Also, I was thankful for the men, women, and cadre who helped me get to that point.

The rest of the semester seemed like a blur. I published my first book, *The Dark Side of the Moon: The Modern Young Man's Search for Himself* that Fall. I was thrilled to see my lofty goal from freshman year come to fruition. I outlined my life in a soundtrack format, describing my life experiences and the people I love in a poetic and honest manner. At its infancy, I wanted to gain understanding over my life and my story. Upon completion, I was constantly embracing everything of what made me, *me*.

2019's conclusion helped me see the rewards of those long nights of brainstorming, writing, and editing. I took full advantage of that year and found myself in an elevated position because of my hard work. I could not have pursued and accomplished my goals without the advice and aid of my friends, mentors, and peers.

They proved that they cared about me by lifting me when I fell to the floor. They talked to me when I had no one else to talk to. They made me smile when all of the world compelled me to frown. Enduring paid great dividends no matter what I told myself during my worst moments. I never seemed to walk alone. Even when I did, I found new ones to walk with. Sometimes you cannot stand alone, you need the help of others to carry you to the end. I found beauty in my struggle against life's evils. I tried my best to do what my loved ones had done for me.

-

Before I knew it the semester was gone and winter break was upon us. New Year's Eve arrived suddenly like it had the year before. I felt about ten years older, satisfied with the overall scope of my life. Fireworks popped off throughout the night as I gazed upon the triumphs and pitfalls of 2019. I was happy, full of gratitude, ready to do it all again. Life was moving ahead, smoothly, swiftly, and successfully. Little did I know that it would change in a snap.

Chapter 8: Quarantined Dreams

Typical days in ROTC included physical training (PT), leadership labs, additional training obligations, and one field training exercise (FTX) in the fall and spring semesters. Most mornings before PT, it is common to see sad cadets trudge to the entrance of the HAC fitness center. Dark humor usually pervades the ride from the dorms to the HAC, continuing upon arrival and Company formation. The routine of warm-up drills, PRT, and military movement drills requires some amount of humor and to laugh at yourself. No college student wants to wake up early to work out and fulfill their responsibilities. *It is rather difficult to balance professionalism when morale is lacking significantly at times.*

I interpret the partial makeup of a successful organization to efficiently balance humor and discipline. A high-performing organization requires firmly established standards and managing flexibility between mission pertinent tasks & administering proper care of its individuals. Mornings before, during, and after PT were a constant fluctuation of these three values: *standards*, *tasks*, and *unit morale*. Leaders in training of any organizational structure often fail at this balance, myself included.

Cadets learn best when failing to effectively balance an organization's needs and mission completion. Team Leader, Squad Leader, Platoon Sergeant, 1st Sergeant... Leadership is both *top-down* and *bottom-up*, it goes both directions. Anyone can contaminate a business, ROTC program, or team from either source. Energy and leadership are just as contagious, a necessary emphasis of any individual within a command structure.

Our small unit composition allows cadets to gain significant leadership experience compared to other ROTC programs. We are trained to balance the academic requirements of Carroll while being in an intensive educational environment (ROTC). Fewer numbers of cadets allow this organization's members to become closer to one another. Yet, close proximity can create internal conflicts rather quickly. Small unit sizes possess the ability to gossip, cause drama, and form rifts between classes and individuals.

After twenty years of trial and error, our company's structure developed to today's current form. Historically, cadets are successful upon exiting Carroll College because of the command structure currently in place. During my four years, it seemed like there was always some form of drama hurting the program. It only takes two with a personal issue, to hinder the development of an organization. I had to learn how to assume my role correctly early on. I failed a lot, often giving misguiding instructions or being confusing in my delivery of instructions. Others have had the same issue in this program and in every organization ever in human history. Assessing the strengths and weaknesses of every leader can dictate how you will lead. Never forget that you can lead from any position. After all, Team Leader is the most important position in a Platoon.

—

Like a blink of an eye, COVID-19 critically damaged the structure of our ROTC program. The remainder of the year increasingly became the unforeseeable future. Immediate effects of the pandemic included severe breaks in personal relationships, accountability within the program, and newfound mental health issues among cadets. One example is from senior cadet, Roxy Ward, who discussed her struggles in taking care of her dogs, a curriculum requirement of Anthrozoology majors at Carroll. She said, "The biggest problem was how the shut-down effected my ability to find one of my dogs who desperately needed a foster home. My personal dogs had an issue with this dog, a border collie. It was difficult to train my dogs properly in service tasks while keeping them physiologically stable."[17]

Our lives during quarantine might have varied from one another but many common aspects remained the same. Anyone in Saints Company asked themselves, *Now what?* The pandemic was confusing, isolating, and detrimental to the successes of all organizations and individuals. The following section is my experience from the wake of the virus to the beginning of the following school year (2020).

—

Upon the opening of the latch door, above the collection of narrow, wooden steps, my brothers and I found this dusty, old barn floor. The second level consisted of cobwebs and their spiders, dirt, grime, and sloppily hammered-in nails. There was a ping pong table sitting at the far end of the room, folded up, crying to be opened.

My brothers and I looked at one another, having a vision for the potential of this barn space. We saw a garage door, the former path for hay to be thrown down to ground level. It was green, like moss in the middle of April. The barn reminded me of a fading star, it was once something rather beautiful, simple in existence, now withering in our physical reality. Despite its current condition we knew there was an opportunity for this black dwarf's proper reclamation.

—

My father and stepmother moved to an eight-acre farm about a week or two after Carroll College closed its doors. Upon my arrival, we packed up our old home, loaded our goods into a U-HAUL, and drove off. They bought a farm in Carnation, thirty miles east of Seattle, laden with green and flowering vegetation. The property sits on a collection of hills, surrounded by small farm buildings. Buildings possessed a large amount of moss, ridden with nails failed to be hammered in correctly.

An obvious home improvement project, we set out to work, building an elevated garden and cleaning out the shop and the other barn buildings. My brothers and I mainly built fences, demolished chicken coops, and pulled out the random stumps scattered throughout the property. My parents intended on buying livestock and growing vegetables that could help sustain our family's food, providing an organic source of nutrition. Most of the high-paying jobs my father offered to us were focused around the future functionality of the farm. The lesser-paying routes of employment were purely for aesthetics and material pleasure.

Our days typically started at eight AM. I would finish a job, go workout in the shop, start another project, and workout in the evening. In the shop, I built a homemade gym using sandbags, plumbing pipes, large rocks, and a small kettlebell. For example, my brother Jack and I constructed a pullup bar, mounting it to the loft above the workout space. We also mounted a punching bag for boxing practice and built a pulley to hoist sandbags. My favorite exercise was the Atlas stone lift. This involved the rapid and repetitive lifting of a sixty-eighty lb. rock for strength and short-term cardio. We put the rocks throughout our property to good use, trying to make the most out of our newly acquired space.

Work heavily involved physical exercise—filling in potholes, loading fallen trees, or chopping wood. In the evening I would come back to the shop, do jump-rope and curl an old tire we found with steel chains. We used the chains as my "bar", curling the tire while my stomach laid flat on top of the loft. This exercise was a painful way to end the day. Yet, I loved to experience physical strain within my fitness dungeon. It was mine, my little world separate from the craziness going on around me.

Exercise became my saving grace during the shut-down. As you can probably tell, school was barely incorporated into my schedule. I lost all focus on my studies for the first month and a half. I emotionally and physically cut myself off from everyone except my brothers and my few friends from high school who came over occasionally. The only enjoyment I found was in exercise, where I could exert my life's frustration into a focused environment.

My gym was created to be dirty, unorthodox, and pseudo-hardcore. We installed a full speaker system where I could blast the loudest metal music I could find in my library. My ears continually rang, my facial hair kept growing, and I was alone despite my world's music. I entered a place of solitude, experiencing depression, and forming great interpersonal agitation. After a few weeks, I started to pick apart the struggles I was facing, beginning to orient myself to my near and far future.

I decided on branching in combat arms in the Army, preferably the Infantry, in an Active-Duty unit. I wanted to join a unit like the 82nd or 101st Airborne. I was even open to the 10th Mountain Division. The path I had chosen, the one that I desired, began to claw back at me. *Why?* It made no sense; I knew this was going to be a very difficult transition for me. Something deep inside kept gnawing at me, wanting more. I began seeking a greater challenge yet again. My newfound goal hit me in the head during one of the many work days outside. Like a badly thrown baseball pitch, it knocked me slightly senseless and jump-started my heart.

Special Forces...Green Berets...Ranger Regiment...

I knew I could do it, no matter what anyone had to say in opposition. Just as my life had been the past few years, it required another massive leap in physical and mental execution. I said to myself, *"Let's go."*

-

I began training like a maniac near the end of the online schoolyear. A bonfire was lit underneath me, everyday into the night I was pushing myself to near exhaustion. You can ask my brothers who would always shake their heads. *You're an idiot, you already worked out today.* I didn't care what anyone in my family had to say, I had to keep going.

I started to see immediate results, beginning to be thankful for the predicament the pandemic put me in. I enjoyed the lone wolf attitude, the ambitions towards my bold dreams. No one believed in me but I did not care, I knew I could make my life happen.

Am I evil? Yes, I fucking am!

-

Despite the joys of free food, family, and friends I had the urge to go back to Montana for my last summer at Carroll. At the time, I needed independence even if it made my life more difficult. I got back to Helena, living in Boromeo over the summer with my friend Dawson. He decided earlier that year that he was going to train for the Navy SEALs upon graduation. In the early days of summer, we began training together while his football regimen began. Workouts were high-rep, 120 lb. sandbag workouts outside, involving sprints, burpees, and pushups.

Dawson had this description of the summer of COVID-19: "It was unique, brutal, and ambitious. It was unique in the fact that it was a completely new living situation, living in Boromeo with a new roommate (Nate). We lived on an empty campus in the middle of summer while everyone was back home enjoying the sun. We were training using an SOF preparation regimen for six days a week for a period of one and a half months. Also, football strength lifting was three times a week, conditioning was twice a week, and I had a full-time job at Pureview administering COVID tests. As roommates, we were ambitious in the fact that while people were at home, especially during COVID, we utilized a comfortable season to get after it. We went on rucks, did high-rep sandbag workouts, ran sprints, and finished them off with jacked-up HIIT circuits."[26]

Our diet consisted of eggs, tuna, couscous, rice, wasabi peas, and quinoa. We lived the cheapest and healthiest lifestyle we possibly could. We became obsessed with our goals, adopting voodoo like practices of drinking shots of clam juice every night. Eventually, Dawson's weight maintenance requirements for football and its opposing style of training began to conflict with our regimen together.

During that summer, I acquired a job at Crossroads fitness in town. I usually opened the business at 3:30 in the morning, beginning my first workout at ten AM. I would rest in the middle of the day or do various errands around town. In the evening I exercised, usually focusing on long-term and short-term cardio by rowing or distance runs. I began integrating high-rep, bodyweight workouts into my regimen. Pullups, body squats, pushups, and box jumps were common exercises I did.

I talk about fitness a lot, especially in this section because it was one of the few activities I could do during the tenure of COVID-19. Besides exercise, during the summer I went on two road trips to Glacier National Park and southern Idaho. I was able to see my roommate from India, Angelo, during the trip to Glacier. My mom, sister, and brother traveled with me all across Idaho. Similar to the trips' iteneraries, most of the activities outside of my daily routine were hiking, running, or shooting. I tried my best to take advantage of the summer and the Montana sun as best as possible.

While we were technically trapped because of the pandemic, I did whatever I could whenever I could. The perspective of taking full advantage of my present circumstance helped me conquer my insecurities during this time. I did not enjoy my life throughout the pandemic. The spring and summer were arduous and incredibly challenging in many aspects.

My dream of going special forces propelled my self-discipline forward. *Discipline* translated directly into the proper prioritization of my daily experience. Unlike the past, my motivations now lasted, like a slow burning fire that seemed to stay alive through all of the seasons.

-

There was a certain euphoria to the summer season, similar to summers in the past. *Germany, Work in the Freezer, India,* and now this year in *Montana*. All incredibly different from each other with shared commonalities. All possessed newfound challenges, leading to an eventual reward in its end. *The sun warms my spirit even though I was feeling down, deprived, and destitute.*

I had reoccurring sleep problems that reminded me of years past. Many nights I would sleep on the couch at the gym or in my car when COVID first entered into the dorm buildings. I ate on a budget, scavenging my way forward through most of the summer. Work was for money towards gas and my summer housing costs. Training was purpose driven, for a newborn dream of pursuing the special forces. I felt fully-prepared for this season, incrementally progressing, gaining toughness every day.

My time at home and my summer in Montana seemed to culminate at the end of July. I had a rather intense week at work and was exhausted overall. My muscles ached and I was trying to begin the next school year as fast as I could. I concluded my second workout for the day by driving up to the

Quarry, at the southern hills of downtown. I stared into the evening sky unsure of what I was doing with my life.

My body was shooting me with pain as I sat on the hood of my car, staring into the valley below. Walking back into my car, I rapidly opened the door, slamming it suddenly. I smacked the wheel of my blueberry-colored Subaru Impreza and said, "Screw it. I'm running a marathon." Like I stated earlier, I was training hard but was not preparing properly for a marathon run. I had full confidence in myself to finish with a solid time even though I had never done distance running extensively. I decided the next week, the Friday before the start of school, I would run my marathon.

On the morning of the race, I woke up early and picked up my friend, Artem, who volunteered to help me throughout the run. I had my supplies packed in my car with various foods, water, and other sources of hydration to accomadate my nutritional needs during the marathon. I began the race by tying my Bob Marley bandana onto my head and putting my headphones on. The run felt like a breeze, like the morning's first caress of wind. I ran and hit my time hacks for the first nine miles.

Due to hunger, I ate too much energy chews on the ninth mile, feeling nauseous for the following three miles. After my half hour of nausea was the greatest runner's high I have ever experienced. Strength, energy, momentum, and drive flooded my veins; my vitality was made wholesome.

In those few miles, I wished this feeling could be placed into a pill so everyone could experience the rush my body had. It was the purest form of euphoria. Running's *drug* was properly sourced when manufactured. Conquering this personal challenge at the finale of this transformative season indicated the amount of necessary pain required to receive grace. I truly believe that you cannot taste *love* if you have not tasted *rejection*. You cannot experience *triumph* when you have never *lost*. *Pain* is the opposite of *grace*; I suffered so I could truly grasp a miniscule moment and its day.

I was made for this moment, for my life. At the source of myself is an individual infected with life's disease. I am illustrated by the insecurities I have obtained. I made who I am, I am who I am. Life is a constant fight for your potential, a test of endurance. Most of the time I want the day to be over with. I am chasing a feeling that tomorrow might be better than today. I cry and whither wishing to be more motivated and stronger the following day.

"I'm not good enough." "I am lazy." "I am not as good as they are." "I have done so much." "I have earned it." In my short life and its minature accomplishments, I know that I cannot succumb to weakness. I am desperate for self-actualization and discovering what I am truly capable of.

"I want to die." Meaning, I want to live everyday like it is my last. Everyone fears death but you should learn to welcome your mortality. I am not there yet but am becoming more liberated by my attempt to accept it.

At about mile eighteen, everyone says you hit the "runner's wall." My experience was not like that at all. I was peaking in my runner's high by mile eighteen, chugging along smoothly, uplifted by not hitting the wall like most people during marathon. All my mile times had been sub-10:30 until mile nineteen. On my route, mile nineteen was near the Costco and Super 1 Foods store at the far reaches of Helena. Almost instantly, my legs and hips locked up, seizing me of my jazz-like motion. At this distance I only desired to finish the race, alike to my desire to fly to Germany. *I had to do it. I had to finish.* This is going to sound corny but failure was not an option.

I kept running and my mile times slowed by fifteen seconds every marker—10:30, 10:45, 11:00... This decline in speed continued till mile twenty-four. By this time, I had no feeling whatsoever in my legs, calves, and hips. Drive got me through to the near-end. I turned off my music by mile twenty-four, practicing self-motivating during my present condition. I seemed to hop forward on the last mile. Every step injected pain from my toes up into my spine, concluding at my forehead. The blisters on my heels and my soles hardened a few miles earlier, now popping, messing with my nerves and present conscience.

Once I saw the finish line, any doubt that could have been in my mind was quickly eliminated. I concluded my marathon, telling myself that I knew what death was like. I was obviously wrong but that didn't stop me from celebrating with a bag of mini-frosted donuts and a cold swim in a nearby river. I wanted to experience the highs and lows of this run once again in the near future. *I used to tell myself that I would never be able to run a marathon. I did it. Check.*

-

About two weeks later, school began and the MSIVs had to make up our canceled summer training during our first weekend of the fall semester. Colleges and Universities in the region met at Fort Harrison for the infamous Operation Agile Leader (OAL) for makeup training. My legs still did not feel one hundred percent by the long weekend's beginning. My classmates and I were not incredibly motivated either. College resumed to a partially in-person format (hybrid classes), especially frustrating because we were out in the hot August sun. We tried our best to take advantage of this training time and Carroll's MSIV class performed rather well.

These were our first steps toward the end, a new beginning for our futures. *I got the branch I wanted.* Rasch and I scored "Most Preferred" for Cadets who put Infantry in their top five branches of choice. This meant we were in the top 3rd of cadets nationwide for this category. *I was thrilled.* Now, the commissioning MSIVs were waiting on assuming senior leadership positions in the program and the completion of our final degree requirements. As you can probably imagine, it was an exciting, scary, and consequential time. Our friends would soon be chasing after their dreams, attempting to take on the world and its malevolent roadblocks. The world did not look the same since we saw each other last spring. It was our final period before the unknown yet again.

.

Chapter 9: The Duality of an Ending

Much of the human spirit is dead, we have deviated from art, literature, music and what makes us beautiful. Mankind has replaced the human spirit with the fallacies and ill-placed concerns of existential influences. Why should fear deter us in our humble quests for glory? The belief of nothing, a void, is formed in the reality of our present circumstance. It is the void of existing humanity currently wrestles with.

My perspectives are a distant essence of wisdom, like only seeing the shadow of the sun. The true form of wisdom is disconnected from the material world. Just like the sun, you cannot stare at it or you will go blind. We have to adapt our eyes to stare at the sun's rays, starting with its shadows, then its light, and finally being able to catch glimpses of it in its entirety.

We can only achieve once we acknowledge this fact by taking a step back from our point in all of time, seeing ourselves from a bird's view. Human and an individual's history is inextricably linked with one another. We can draw from lessons of the past, apply innovations in the present, and progress in the future. Progression is not always positive, sometimes you make the wrong choice even if your will desires an output of grace.

Time will always move along regardless of what you have to say. Upon your life's end you will come to terms with your brief stay on Earth. Before we cross into the transcendental plain, we must learn to walk around our brutish world. The difference between the satisfactory and the proficient is the acquired ability to run instead. What would life be if you could only walk?

The next year proceeded like the clicking of the fast-forward button on a remote. Many of us were fine-tuning the next evolution of our lives. Some were getting married, some were moving away, and some had no idea what they were going to do next. Many of the previously infinite days, classes, and obligations were more manageable; we felt more adequately prepared for the next few years ahead. Life had been so uncertain within the past year that my class and I seemed equipped for any sudden changes to plans (even though sometimes it made us quite hostile).

Carroll College adopted a hybrid classroom policy after the shut-down. Once the vaccine(s) became more readily accessible, the concerns over COVID-19 began to steadily dwindle. Our PT schedule switched during the week to two separate PT sessions, splitting up the upper and lowerclassmen. Lab now factored in cadets needing to quarantine or those suddenly getting sick.

Despite being present on campus, Saints Company encountered now unforeseen protocols and circumstances. Whereas the previous spring had a stay-at-home mandate, now Carroll College as a whole needed to establish a baseline system for the pandemic, effecting the close-knit relationships within the program.

As far as lessons learned, *planning for the worst* should have been a priority among cadre members, cadets, and faculty at the school. We often neglect the unforeseen and the consequences when being overconfident. Many cadets felt that our lack of planning and protocol establishment slowed the programs progress down significantly. The MSIVs came to the conclusion that their present circumstance could be mitigated by adapting their leadership styles and skills towards this "hybrid" situation.

We now had to assume the worst and adjust communication between cadets, cadre, and planning for training events. This was only a continuation of the changes seen in the previous ten months. Incorporating fresh tactics towards the program's proper function was necessary, forcing issues to be solved quickly and differently than in year's past. Such adjustments were seen globally, at the systemic, communal, and individual levels. COVID-19 slowed the world down but Saints Company kept treading forward despite the severity of the pandemic and its effects.

-

Similar to the fate of all college students, the future began to appear on the immediate horizon. Instead of leaving our family's home, some of us were going directly into the Army or pursuing additional goals as well. This chapter characterizes the end and the beginning of a certain stage in an officer's life. Just as people experience drastic changes in life, this is similarly felt for cadets.

Cadets are forced into a transitional period upon arrival. They are a cross between soldier and student, youth and adult, forced to decipher dreams and potential realities. While ROTC is not the most difficult coursework, asking young adults to figure out major life decisions is a lot to ask of a young individual.

This is why the *past, present, and future* are given to advise current and future officers through initial self-reflective feedback. Transition is particularly difficult for the average person but is especially unique to someone in the armed forces. In the following pages, many cadre, veterans, and current service members give their two cents for the upcoming future.

These quotes are sourced from NCOs and Officers of the past and present, for a wholistic section of advice. In conclusion, the chapter ends with advice from each of the MSIVs at Carroll College (2021) for future commissioned officers in this ROTC program.

Some of these voices have not made themselves present to you. In fact, you will not know all of them, despite their direct or indirect influences upon you. As time ticks on, these names will fade away like our earthly forms inevitably do so. This is fine, this is the greater community you are a part of, men and women of the armed forces. Words of the past should never be forgotten for there is wisdom in all places, people, and periods of time.

Regardless of your role or motivations during your military career, these individuals have your back. Rested upon the bedrock of their experiences, all offer quotes for life and your obligation of service.

Successes and failures will riddle your life just as it has carved itself into mine. We are all beggars of wisdom, ambitious students of the human experience. Learn from them, hear what they have to say...They have your best outcome in mind.

-

Question: "If you have one piece of advice for my MSIV class about to get commissioned, what would you say?"

SFC Robert Cassidy, MTARNG

Former: 11C Mortarman; Recruit Training Coordinator for MTARNG; NCOIC for Carroll College ROTC from 2013-2018; current 42A Battalion S1 for the 1-189th GSAV

"Work together, finish together. That's huge moving forward in your careers. Look out for your soldiers. Soldier care is number one, get to know them because you are not better than the lowest rank in your platoon. These relationships are valuable and essential so maintain approachability with your soldiers. Let them come talk to you and be motivated to listen to what they have to say. Be adaptable to new situations. Have an open-mind to new perspectives and ideas for your future and day-day life."

2LT Otis Smith, IARNG

Current: 70A Health Services Administrative Officer

Carroll College AROTC Class of 2020 – Degree in Business Management

"Take a step back, take a breath, does it really matter in the grand scheme of things? If you are upset, is that really going to change your life? Carry on, roll with it. Anything bad that happened to you probably happened for a reason. I primarily used this perspective near the end of my ROTC career. I can get upset about what's wrong but it's a waste of my time to."

MSG Travis Hambrick, Special Mission Unit (Retired)

Former: Active-Duty 2/75th Ranger BN Sniper Section Leader and PSG; HHC 75th Regimental Reconnaissance Detachment specializing in small-unit tactics; Enlisted Special Mission Unit Member (E8) from 1991-2015

Sam Hambrick's Father

"Focus on the soldiers that you are assigned to lead, they are your number one priority. Be tough and fair in your leadership! Always remember that the most valuable asset the US Army has is Soldiers!"[30]

CPT Christopher Clark, MTARNG

Former: 90A Logistics Officer; Full-time National Guard MOB Project Officer; OIC for Carroll College ROTC from 2019-2021; current ORSA systems analyst (O-4) at the National Guard Headquarters in Arlington, VA

"Never underestimate the power of being a kind person."[27]

CPL Warren G. Teafatiller, 3rd BN 5th Marines, USMC (Retired)

Former: Active Corporal (E4) Rifleman specializing in counter-terrorism operations in the Philippines and Central & South America from 1990-1994

<u>Relative of Nate</u>

"Never ask anyone to do anything that you wouldn't be willing to do yourself. With that in mind you can make decisions when they matter most. Know that mission accomplishment always comes first and foremost. Be strong, be confident, and never second guess yourself! If you do this, you will earn the respect from all hands."[34]

CW2 Bollinger, MTARNG

Former: 13A Field Artillery Officer; OIC for Carroll College ROTC from 2003-2006 (LTCOL); INDO-PACOM & CENTCOM National Guardsman State Partnership Program Coordinator; current Assistant J1 to the 208th RTI in Helena, MT

"I've been in the Army for 29 years in Active Duty, AGR, Reserve, and National Guard roles. The opportunities in the military are endless. Keep your eyes wide open, look for opportunities. There are tons of life-changing paths that you didn't even know existed; you should explore all that are available to you whether you stay in or not. You have no idea how your path is going to unfold beyond the next 2-3 years."

SSG Courtney Sizemore, MTARNG

Former: 68W Combat Medic; Medical Care Training NCO; 68W Instructor; NCOIC for Carroll College ROTC from 2018-2020; current 68W HHC Readiness NCO for the 1-189th GSAV in Helena, MT

"Ensure that you find a mentor at your first duty station. Always ensure you listen to your Platoon Sergeant for guidance."[32]

MSG Gary Marshall, 160th SOAR (Retired)

Former: Active-Duty 11B Infantryman, 11C Mortarman, and 15T Flight Medic with the 101st Airborne and the 506th Aviation; 16W-S Special Forces Medic with Task Force 160th from 1985-2005

<u>Friend of Nate</u>

"Listen to your senior NCOs, don't jump into it thinking your rank means more than them. Also, never ask someone to do something that you would never be willing to do yourself. I have run

into officers thinking that they are above all the required tasks. As a 2LT listen to your E6s and E7s, they have been there, done their tours, and know how the military properly functions. Their experiences are real, once combat actually occurs you don't know how you're going to react. It is different to be around your NCOs rather than officers. Don't have a big head."[31]

1LT James Infanger, MTARNG
Former: Active-Duty 11B Infantryman in the 82nd Airborne; 11B 1-158th Cavalry Squadron; 11B 1-157th Infantry Regiment; Strategic Exercise Planner for NORAD & USNORTHCOM, Platoon Sergeant for Fort Carson Warrior Transition Battalion; and current S2 Officer for the 1-163rd Combined Arms Battalion Officer (02)

"In your career, take calculated risks and punch above your perceived weight (wisely)… meaning, don't get comfortable… constantly consider how you can increase your relevancy and dynamism, take on more responsibility than you might want, gain experiences outside of your comfort zone and do the things that scare the hell out of you... physically and mentally, and thrive…You will surprise yourself more often than not and you will open doors and build networks you never realized were there."[31]

2LT Parker Perry, WARNG
Current: 35A Intelligence Officer at Fairchild Airforce Base and Sheriff's Deputy in Spokane County, WA
Carroll College AROTC Class of 2020 – Degree in Business Management

"Just be you, be humble and display humility. Take criticism and address your weaknesses as best as you can. I think my experience so far has benefitted me positively because of the difficulties I have had to face early on in my civilian and military careers. I realized very quickly how much I needed to learn how to properly care for my soldiers. Its application to law enforcement could not be more direct. Don't be afraid to swallow your pride, all of you need to step up to the plate and lead. You are all different in your own ways, so have no apprehensions towards the future. Figure out how to deal with it and press forward."

ENS Angelo Di Mondo, USS Iwo Jima, USN
Current: Surface Warfare Officer (O1, SWO) in Norfolk, VA
Rutgers NROTC Class of 2020 – Degree in Industrial Engineering
Friend and Roommate of Nate in New Delhi

"Stay open-minded and be intellectually curious in your studies. In your early period as an officer, you need to develop your professional competencies necessary for your first duty assignment until you have the ability to lead effectively. This is not merely being satisfactory but excelling in all of your pursuits and areas of assessment. Read, get physically fit, and challenge yourself."[28]

SFC Matt Sonsteng, MTARNG
Former: 13B Artilleryman; 31B Military Policeman; Temporary Full-Time Duty for State Level & Regional Support Group Operations; current NCOIC for Carroll College ROTC (2021-)

"Don't get discouraged with where your career takes you, capitalize upon any opportunities that are available. Failure does not define where you can go, it is a chance for you to overcome challenges. You never know what blessings are ahead of you, always go with your gut."[33]

CPT Mark Thompson, MTARNG
Former: 15P Aviation Operations Specialist (E4); OIC for Carroll College ROTC from 2016-2019; current 15A Aviation Officer in the 1-189th GSAV in Helena, MT
Carroll College Class of 2007 – Degree in Sociology

"When you go to your first unit as a 2nd LT, know that everyone in the room is smarter than you. Heavily rely on your PSG because they have all the experience. Know you are in charge, own every decision, whether good or bad, but go back to your PSG and have them help you make those difficult decisions. Utilize every available resource of experience to aid in guiding you along. By the time that you become the Company Commander, you want to be the smartest person in the room"

COL Patrick Nugent, MTARNG (Retired)
Former: 91A Ordnance Officer; 90A Logistics Officer; OIC for Carroll College ROTC from 2000-2003; Commander of the 1889th Regional Support Group, 495th Combat Sustainment Support Battalion, 495th Motor Transportation Battalion, and MTARNG Chief of Staff (06) from 1988-2018

"Carrol College is a tremendous program. As a small Cadet Corps, you are able to make much more independent decisions and are trained effectively to self-motivate. This will help you tremendously as a newly Commissioned Officer in the Army"

-

Question: *"If you have one piece of advice for current and future cadets wanting to accomplish what you did while at Carroll, what would you say?"*

CDT Zach Brandt
Major: Biochemistry & Biology
Commissioning as a 70B Health Services Officer in the MTARNG and Attending Creighton University's Medical School in the Fall of 2021

"Keep your eyes on the prize—life is bigger than the things you're going to do here. All the stuff that is easily appealing is not rewarding in the end. It's good to focus on the decisions that will better yourself in the long run. Preparation for the real world is important, it is easy to forget the

privileges you have during these brief four years. One mistake can cost you everything and the consequences are always worth considering before action."

CDT Trevor Drinville

Major: Mathematics & Economics

Commissioning as a 25A Signal Officer in the MTARNG

"Keep on keeping on—life will get better; you will make it out alive. Never forget that someone out there has a life much worse than you. You are fortunate to be in the position you are in."

CDT Daniel Guthrie

Major: Civil Engineering

Commissioning as a hopeful 12A Engineering Officer in the MTARNG in the Winter of 2021

"Don't stress too much, you're always in a better position than you think. Prepare for your obligations while not being discouraged by the stresses of life."

CDT Sam Hambrick

Major: Elementary Education

Commissioning as a hopeful 90A Logistics Officer in the AK ARNG in the Spring of 2022

"My advice for future cadets would be to be a sponge and be a yes man. You are not going to gain experience just by being told what to do, volunteer to do things, step outside of your comfort zone. Invest in the program and your peers. The more you invest in the program and your peers the better officer and person you will be! I have met some of the best people in my life in Carroll's ROTC program and I am going to miss them but I am so excited to see where they go in life and I know I have life-long friends in them."[29]

CDT Tori Lahrman

Major: International Business

Commissioning as an Active-Duty 42B Human Resources Officer

"Be a sponge, absorb everything you can. Don't be afraid to fail hard and fail fast. You will succeed if you persevere. Also, don't forget to bring a flag to a flag folding class."

CDT Jacob Rasch

Major: Sociology

Commissioning as an Active-Duty 11A Infantry Officer

"Self-study is an important discipline to master. There is so much more to the world and to your job than you realize. You can never know or prepare too much. Doctrine can only give you so much information so think outside of the box."

CDT Roxy Ward

Major: Anthrozoology

Commissioning as a hopeful 42B Human Resources Officer in the Army Reserves in the Spring of 2022

"Be ready to learn, absorb the advice you are given. You can change how you can enact it in the future. Be willing to listen, you're going to learn easier through seeing how other people make mistakes. Not everyone needs to have 24/7 staff duty to grow as an individual."

CDT Nate Smith

Major: Political Science

Commissioning as an Active-Duty 11A Infantry Officer

*"My advice to you is simple: **SEEK AND DESTROY!** You have one chance to take advantage of your time here, don't waste a moment of it. If at any point you realize you are not satisfied with your life's results, attack your dreams every single day. I believe that you can go a lot further than you think you can."*

Appendix

Chapter 1: The Mount St. Charles SATC

1 Swartout, Robert R. "Chapter 1." Essay. In *Bold Minds & Blessed Hands: the First Century of Montana's Carroll College*. Helena, MT: Carroll College, 2009.

Chapter 2: The Good Ship Carroll

2 Carroll College Newspaper. "Navy Aviation Cadet Training Detachment." *The Prospector*, February 26, 1943.

3 J.A. Swanson Agency, Inc. Letter to Charmon Pentecost. Response to "The Old Salty Prospector" Newsletter Regarding V5 or V12, 2002.

4 V-12A, and Paul Verdon, Chronology of the U.S. Navy at Carroll College, Helena, Montana, In World War II § (1945).

5 Young, Durand. "2003 Reunion Planning to Begin." *The Old Salty Prospector*. February 2002, Vol. VI edition, sec. No. 1.

6 Young, Durand. "The Good Ship Carroll." *Montana Sheriff Magazine*, October 1996.

Chapter 3: Early Days

7 Carroll College Department of Military Science. "Cadet Kilbreath Falls for Airborne." *ROTC News: "Saints to the Front"*. May 2003, Vol. 2 edition, sec. Issue 5.

8 Carroll College. "Carroll College Announces Dean's List." *Independent Record*. February 9, 2002.

9 Mapston, Austin. "Army ROTC Program up and Running at Carroll." *The Prospector*. February 11, 2002, Vol. 85 edition, sec. No. IV.

10 Miller, Trisha. "The Women of ROTC." *Montana Kaimin*. February 22, 2002.

11 Nugent, Patrick, and Nathaniel Smith. Interview with COL Patrick Nugent: Former Carroll College OIC. E-Mail, 19 APR 2021.

12 Platt, Carrie-Anne. "ROTC Comes to Carroll as Full-Time Program in Fall 2001." *The Prospector*. April 9, 2001, Vol. 84 edition, sec. No. VI.

13 Thompson, Mark, and Nathaniel Smith. Interview with CPT Mark Thompson: Former Cadet and OIC of Carroll College. Personal, 04 MAR 2021.

14 Tode, Laura. "First Carroll ROTC Grad Confident." *Independent Review*. October 7, 2002.

15 CW2 Bollinger, and Nathaniel Smith. Interview with CW2 Bollinger: Former Carroll College OIC. Personal, 23 MAR 2021.

16 Synness, Dan. "ROTC Cadet Synness Jumps at Chance to Attend Prestigious Army Basic Airborne Course." *Carroll College Prospector*. September 16, 2002, Vol. 86 edition, sec. No. 1.

Chapter 4: Preceding the Unknown

17 Cassidy, SFC Robert, and Nathaniel Smith. Interview with SFC Cassidy: Former Carroll College NCOIC. Personal, 26 MAR 2021.

18 Perry, Parker, and Nathaniel Smith. Interviews with former Carroll College Cadets. Personal, 22 MAR 2021.

19 Smith, Otis, and Nathaniel Smith. Interviews with former Carroll College Cadets. Personal, 26 MAR 2021.

Chapter 6: The Void

20 Drinville, Trevor, and Nathaniel Smith. Interviews with Carroll College ROTC MSIVs. Personal, 04 MAR 2021.

21 Rasch, Jacob, and Nathaniel Smith. Interviews with Carroll College ROTC MSIVs. Personal, 05 MAR 2021

Chapter 7: Second Chance

22 Brandt, Zachary, and Nathaniel Smith. Interviews with Carroll College ROTC MSIVs. Personal, 04 MAR 2021.

23 Guthrie, Daniel, and Nathaniel Smith. Interviews with Carroll College ROTC MSIVs. Personal, 19 MAR 2021.

24 Lahrman, Victoria, and Nathaniel Smith. Interviews with Carroll College ROTC MSIVs. Personal, 05 MAR 2021.

Chapter 8: Quarantined Dreams

25 Ward, Roxanne, and Nathaniel Smith. Interviews with Carroll College ROTC MSIVs. Personal, 31 MAR 2021.

26 Zebarth, Dawson, and Nathaniel Smith. Interview with My Roommate During COVID-19. Personal, 06 APR 2021.

Chapter 9: The Duality of an Ending

27 Clark, CPT Christopher, and Nathaniel Smith. Interview with CPT Clark: Former Carroll College OIC. Personal, 06 APR 2021.

28 Di Mondo, ENS Angelo, and Nathaniel Smith. Interview over Our Experience in New Delhi. Personal, 05 APR 2021.

29 Hambrick, Sam, and Nathaniel Smith. Interviews with Carroll College ROTC MSIVs. Personal, 20 APR 2021.

30 Hambrick, MSG Travis, and Nathaniel Smith. Interviews with Veterans of the Armed Forces for "Enduring". E-Mail, 19 APR 2021.

31 Infanger, 1LT James, and Nathaniel Smith. Interview with an Infantryman for Life: 1LT James Infanger for "Enduring". E-mail, 20 APR 2021.

32 Marshall, MSG Gary, and Nathaniel Smith. Interviews with Veterans of the Armed Forces for "Enduring". Personal, 07 APR 2021.

33 Sizemore, SSG Courtney, and Nathaniel Smith. Interview with SSG Sizemore: Former Carroll College NCOIC. E-Mail, 08 APR 2021.

34 Sonsteng, SFC Matthew, and Nathaniel Smith. Interview with SFC Sonsteng: Current Carroll College NCOIC. Personal, 06 APR 2021.

35 Teafatiller, CPL Warren, and Nathaniel Smith. Interviews with Veterans of the Armed Forces for "Enduring". E-Mail, 30 MAR 2021.

Other Contributors

Chapter 5: Gaze Into the Unknown

36 Knott, Matthew, and Nathaniel Smith. Interview with a Former High School Teacher at ECHS. Personal, 08 APR 2021.

37 Lakes, Cameron, and Nathaniel Smith. Interview with Cameron Lakes: Friend, Classmate, Activist, and Teammate. Personal, 12 APR 2021.

Ingram Content Group UK Ltd.
Milton Keynes UK
UKHW050036190423
420355UK00004B/121